MW00780263

What You're Made For

What You're Re Made For

Powerful Life Lessons from My Career in Sports

George Raveling
and **Ryan Holiday**

Foreword by Michael Jordan

Portfolio | Penguin

Portfolio / Penguin
An imprint of Penguin Random House LLC
1745 Broadway, New York, NY 10019
penguinrandomhouse.com

Most Portfolio books are available at a discount when purchased in quantity for sales promotions or corporate use. Special editions, which include personalized covers, excerpts, and corporate imprints, can be created when purchased in large quantities. For more information, please call (212) 572-2232 or email specialmarkets@penguinrandomhouse.com. Your local bookstore can also assist with discounted bulk purchases using the Penguin Random House corporate Business-to-Business program. For assistance in locating a participating retailer, email B2B@penguinrandomhouse.com.

Book design by Alissa Rose Theodor

Library of Congress Control Number: 2024950499
ISBN 9780593852972 (hardcover)
ISBN 9780593852989 (ebook)

Printed in the United States of America
1st Printing

The authorized representative in the EU for product safety and compliance is Penguin Random House Ireland, Morrison Chambers, 32 Nassau Street, Dublin D02 YH68, Ireland, https://eu-contact.penguin.ie.

This book is dedicated to my wife, Delores Akins, my son, Mark, my daughter, Litisha, and to Kimati Ramsey.

Contents

FOREWORD BY MICHAEL JORDAN   ix

INTRODUCTION   xiii

To Be a Trailblazer   1

To Listen and Learn   14

To Seek Out Wisdom   23

To Struggle   33

To Study Books   44

To Dispense Love   54

To Serve Others   60

To Keep Hope Alive   66

To Be a Friend   80

To Build Your Team   89

To Tell the Truth   100

To Win the Day   113

To Reach Your Outer Limits   124

To Bring People with You   132

To Create Order from Chaos   139

To Be a Blessing   146

To Grow a Coaching Tree   155

To Be an Answer   163

To Be a Good Steward   169

To Change the World   177

To Live   187

Foreword

George Raveling is an unsung hero in my life. Our relationship goes back forty years and he's truly been a mentor and a friend to me since our paths first crossed.

I met George when I was twenty-one years old, when he was an assistant coach for the Olympic men's basketball team and I was a skinny junior at the University of North Carolina, about to turn pro and trying out for the team that would compete at the 1984 Olympic Games in Los Angeles. George was a bridge between us players and Coach Bobby Knight. Right away, George was a comfort—a coach who knew how to relate to players and knew the game of basketball inside and out. He smoothed the path for my Olympic teammates on our way to a gold medal. George was the glue that held the team together and he doesn't get the credit he deserves.

Then there's the origin of my partnership with Nike. There are all kinds of stories out there, but George is truly the reason I signed with Nike. As I've said before, I was all in for Adidas. George preached for Nike, and I listened—reluctantly at first. George is the one who convinced me to take what is now an infamous meeting at Tony Roma's in Los Angeles and, well, the rest is history. My relationship with George is what made me feel comfortable signing with Nike. If not for George, there would be no Air Jordan.

In just three months, George was there for two life-changing moments for me—winning my first Olympic gold and signing my first shoe deal with Nike.

Over the years, while I was playing in the NBA, I stayed in close touch with George. He not only made a tremendous impact on me as a coach with his knowledge of the game but also with his ability to listen and be a good sounding board. I've gotten a lot of great, important advice from George. When I started my Michael Jordan Flight School basketball camp, which we held in Santa Barbara for years, George was the obvious choice for me to bring on board as the director. He wouldn't sign on until he was sure we'd be doing the camp the right way—and that I would be there every day. Later, we did a camp for adults—Senior Flight School—and George was instrumental in making that a success too.

What an amazing life George has led and what a role model he is. As the first Black coach in the ACC, the first Black head coach in the then Pac-8, and a founder of the Black Coaches Association, George paved the way and, again, does not get the credit that I feel he deserves.

He's been so influential to so many—including me—and seen

the best and the worst of this world during his incredible life. I'm proud to call George a mentor and a friend. And I'm glad he's telling his story and sharing his life lessons. We can all learn from him.

Michael Jordan

Introduction

Often a very old man has no other proof
of his long life than his age.

—SENECA

I n 1937, the year I was born, the life expectancy of a Black male
was just forty-eight years.

It was a world of stark contrasts—of groundbreaking inno-
vation and entrenched inequality. As I took my first breath, a
thirty-five-year-old cartoonist named Walt Disney was releasing
Snow White and the Seven Dwarfs, the world's first full-length an-
imated feature film. Across the Atlantic, a terrible war was breaking out and Pablo Picasso was putting the finishing touches on his
haunting, heartbreaking anti-war mural, *Guernica*. In sports, Joe
Louis, the "Brown Bomber," became the heavyweight champion
of the world, one of the few victories in an age of setbacks for
Black people.

The Golden Gate Bridge had just opened, a marvel of engi-
neering towering over the San Francisco skyline. Meanwhile, in-
ventors were shaping the future: Chester Carlson was pioneering

the photocopier, László Bíró was perfecting the ballpoint pen, Edwin H. Land was laying the foundation for the Polaroid camera, and Henry W. Altorfer had just invented and patented the electric clothes dryer, an advancement that would replace hand-cranked dryers and forever change the rhythm of household chores.

But for African Americans, it was a world of segregation and discrimination; the odds were stacked against a kid like me from day one. We faced systemic barriers in every aspect of life: education, employment, housing, health care, voting. We lived apart. We were made to use different facilities. We were denied basic rights and dignities. The bleak stage was set: a life of poverty, hardship, and struggle, one cut short by the harsh realities of racism and inequality.

Not that I was thinking about any of this as a child.

But it was in the air.

The hushed whispers and somber faces delivering news of what happened to a neighbor or some extended family member. So were the air raid sirens, blackout curtains, and duck-and-cover drills at school, daily reminders of a world at war. The echoes of the tolling church bells, the beautiful funeral hymns, and the slow-moving processions; the well-dressed men and women, dignified despite it all; artistic flourishes on a life that was fleeting, cruel, over in an instant.

The dark shadow of mortality had always loomed large, but when I was nine, it came right up to our doorstep. My dad—a man of his era, confined by the societal and racial constraints that defined our existence—died of a heart attack when he was forty-nine years old, a tragically ordinary fate for Black men in those days. He had worked hard to support us. He was a groom for wealthy horse owners, often sleeping in the stables among the horses he tended because he couldn't afford to commute to and from the track every day.

His passing marked the first time I truly understood the fragility of life. The suddenness of it, the way a life so central to mine could be extinguished in an instant, haunted me. It was a lesson in mortality that would stay with me, shaping how I viewed every subsequent challenge.

It was then just my mom and me in a small apartment at the corner of New Jersey and Florida Avenues in Washington, D.C., above a store called Shep's Market. On the second floor, there were three apartments. We had a kitchen, a little living room, and one bedroom with a bed we both slept in. Everyone in the building shared one bathroom, with a bathtub, sink, and toilet. We had to figure out how to share it, but we managed.

In those days, Washington, D.C., was 73 percent Black. That's how it eventually got the nickname Chocolate City. Most of these folks had fled the even harsher conditions of the Deep South, seeking a better life. In the nation's capital, they could make a decent living in the shadows of institutions like the White House and the Capitol, providing the cheap yet indispensable labor that kept the governmental machinery running. The irony: we were integral to the city's functioning, yet marginal in its society.

The vibrancy of the neighborhood was a sharp contrast to the stark inequalities that defined our daily existence. Yet within it there was an undeniable sense of community—a shared struggle that bound us together, even as we navigated the harsh realities of segregation.

My mom, like many others, juggled three jobs to make ends meet. She would walk four miles to get downtown, and her parting words to me each day, "Don't you leave this building," were not just instructions but a plea for safety in a world that was not kind to little Black boys.

The intersection of New Jersey and Florida Avenues was a busy one, teeming with life and the rhythmic flow of city traffic. From my window, I would spend countless hours observing the world outside. The street below bustled with cars honking and streetcars clanging as they made their way through the city. The streetcars moved with a mechanical certainty that fascinated me. Each had its own unique number, a detail that caught my interest and that I tracked in a small notebook. Whenever a streetcar glided past, I'd write down its number and the time of day. When that streetcar came back around, I'd note the return time. This routine was my little way of engaging with the outside world, a way to order the chaos that often surrounded me.

One day when I was thirteen years old, I walked into the kitchen and my mom was pouring a bag of sugar down the drain. That bag of sugar could have lasted us two or three months. I told my grandma—we called her "Dear"—about it, and she'd noticed my mom was doing a lot of strange stuff too. I can't exactly recall what the breaking point was, but one day my mom just disappeared. Nobody knew where she went. Nobody thought to explain anything to me. Finally, they tracked her down and she was up in Boston. She had been committed to St. Elizabeth Mental Institution, where she remained for the rest of her life.

Despite these circumstances, which had made me, on top of everything else, effectively an orphan, despite the despair that loomed over my childhood, despite the bleak statistics and low expectations—I survived. Though the universe seemed to deal me a losing hand in a rigged, short game, I stand here at eighty-seven at the time of this writing, still playing, with multiple lifetimes' worth of experiences and accomplishments.

I was the first person in my family to go to college, receiving a basketball scholarship to Villanova University, where I was just the second Black player in the program's history.

I met several U.S. presidents: Gerald Ford, Ronald Reagan, Jimmy Carter, Bill Clinton, and Harry S. Truman, who gave me a signed copy of his autobiography.

I was Wilt Chamberlain's right-hand man for one incredible summer. I shook hands with Muhammad Ali. I walked up to the great Sammy Davis Jr. in a restaurant once and started to introduce myself. Before I could get a word out, he looked up at me—all five feet, five inches of him—and said, "George Raveling!" To this day, I do not know how he could have possibly known who I was.

I stood alongside Dr. Martin Luther King Jr. on the steps of the Lincoln Memorial during the March on Washington, and after he delivered his historic "I Have a Dream" speech, Dr. King handed me his typewritten notes, which I've preserved (much more on this in the chapter "To Keep Hope Alive").

I was the first Black basketball coach at Villanova, the University of Maryland, Washington State University, and the University of Iowa.

I've coached Olympic gold medal teams and Hall of Fame players.

I played against Jerry West before the NBA logo was his silhouette, traveled to Peking before it was called Beijing, worked with Phil Knight before Nike had a stock price, and coached Michael Jordan before he had a signature shoe.

There are coaches who have won more than I have. There are coaches who were more highly paid—a *lot* more highly paid. There are coaches who became celebrities. Still, I've been inducted into both the Naismith Memorial Basketball Hall of Fame and the National Collegiate Basketball Hall of Fame. That was never what motivated me, never what I thought my job was. In fact, the door of my office never read "Head Basketball Coach." It read, at my direction:

GEORGE RAVELING.
EDUCATOR.

I never expected that they'd end up making a movie about me, but they did, and it was nominated for multiple Golden Globes. In fact, the Oscar-winning actor and filmmaker Ben Affleck tells the story of flying to meet Michael Jordan to get his blessing to make the movie *Air*, about his journey to signing with Nike in 1984. Michael had two conditions: Viola Davis had to play his mom, and "George Raveling needs to be included in the story. He's vital. I wouldn't be at Nike without him."

Today, when I see him or other players (some I coached, many I never did) like Charles Barkley, Patrick Ewing, or Dirk Nowitzki; when I get a call from coaches like John Calipari, Doc Rivers, or Shaka Smart; or when I hear from readers of a newsletter I started, *The Daily Coach*, we don't just talk about basketball. We talk about life. We talk about history.

And, boy, have I lived through some history.

In my lifetime, President Franklin D. Roosevelt steered the nation through the Great Depression, the attack on Pearl Harbor, and most of World War II. President Harry S. Truman made the decision to drop atomic bombs on Hiroshima and Nagasaki. The Civil Rights Movement gained momentum during the presidency of Dwight D. Eisenhower. The assassination of John F. Kennedy shocked the nation. Lyndon B. Johnson signed the Civil Rights

Act and the Voting Rights Act into law. Richard Nixon resigned in the wake of the Watergate scandal. And Barack Obama became the first African American president of the United States.

I've lived through the Korean War and Vietnam (I served two years in the army), the fall of the Berlin Wall on television, the collapse of the Soviet Union, the economic boom and the political scandals of the Clinton years, and the tumultuous presidency of George W. Bush, defined by the 9/11 attacks and the wars in Afghanistan and Iraq.

I've seen the entire space age unfold, from the launch of the first satellite into orbit when I was twenty years old, to humans walking on the moon, to the construction of the International Space Station. There's been major health crises like the crack epidemic, polio, the Asian flu pandemic, the AIDS crisis, and COVID-19. The rise of television, air travel, the interstate highway system, suburbs, and fast food. The invention of the internet, mobile phones, credit cards, email, personal computers, GPS, and Wi-Fi.

I have lived not one life, but many. At the age of fifty-seven, I was blindsided in a two-car collision that left me with a broken pelvis, nine broken ribs, a broken clavicle, a collapsed lung, and bleeding in my chest. Doctors told me 95 percent of people in similar accidents die. Once again, I survived. Once again, I defied death and probability.

I lived another life since that accident, a bonus life, as I've come to see it. I retired from coaching basketball after a twenty-two-year career. I guess I could have lived out my twilight years in a comfortable chair. Instead, I joined Nike as the director of international basketball and brought together the top high school players from around the world, discovering and bringing international stars like Yao Ming and Dirk Nowitzki to the NBA. I would serve as an adviser to the Los Angeles Clippers for over a decade and consult with the 2008 Redeem Team, which won a gold medal in Beijing. To this day, I'm writing and coaching and educating because it keeps me going, it gives me purpose, and it's fun.

It would be impossible for a person to experience all that I have and not become a little philosophical. By *philosophical*, I don't mean abstract or esoteric. I mean it in the practical, reflective sense. At some point, it hit me that the sweep of history I'd experienced was as vast as the books and biographies I've always loved to read. That I had lived a life far bigger than the imagination of that kid staring out the window over New Jersey and Florida Avenues. That I would become older than pretty much everyone I ever met. And at some point—not unlike the way it was impossible as a child to get away from the sense that life is short—I couldn't help but ask questions like:

Why me?

Why was I spared when so many others weren't?

Why was I gifted with this extra time?

And what do I do with this gift?

This kind of introspection isn't merely a luxury of age; it's a necessity, a way to reconcile the randomness of existence with the purpose I sought. I realized that the answers weren't in the grand events, but in the quiet moments, in the decisions made when no one was watching, in the way I chose to face each new day.

Of course, you don't have to have a life like mine to ask these sorts of questions. These might be questions that you've asked yourself at some point. Maybe not in those exact words. But in quiet moments or in the face of life's challenges and triumphs, you've probably asked yourself questions like: Why am I here?

What is my purpose? What unique contribution am I meant to make in this world?

For me, these questions—and their answers—didn't come all at once. For a while, they lurked somewhere pretty far in the back of my mind. But slowly, over a couple of decades, they came to the forefront. And eventually, they merged into a single, all-encompassing question. I still have the notebook in which I first wrote it down:

What was I made for?

From the harsh streets of Chocolate City to the hallowed halls of the Basketball Hall of Fame and beyond, my life has been an improbable series of unexpected opportunities, hard-fought battles, and lessons learned.

This book is not a memoir. I was never interested in writing one of those. It is an exploration of purpose and meaning. It is stories and lessons to inspire, to challenge, and to provoke thought about the roles we are each called to play in this complex, beautiful life.

This is not just my story, but a quest to understand the essence of what it means to be made for something more, to defy the odds, and to carve out a destiny that transcends all expectations and limitations.

It is a call to reflect on your own path, to question the arbitrary limitations placed upon you, and to dare to dream of a life beyond statistics and societal expectations.

As you turn these pages, I invite you to confront the whys of your existence, to question what it means to live a life of intention and meaning, to ask . . .

What was I made for?

This is not a question with a simple answer, nor is it one that can be answered for you by anyone else. It is a deeply personal inquiry. It is a lifelong quest that requires introspection, an examination of your talents, your interests, your values, and your experiences. It requires courage, a willingness to step into the unknown and beyond the limits and expectations that have been set for you. The stereotypes and statistics that may be placed upon you, your race, your gender, your background, or your circumstances.

You have to be willing to dream big. You have to allow yourself to believe that you were made for something special, something unique, something that only you can bring into this world. You have to let yourself hear that still, quiet voice within, the one that whispers of a higher calling, a greater contribution.

In the pages that follow, you'll discover how to carve out your own unique path, even when conventional wisdom or societal expectations push you in a different direction. We'll delve into the art of maintaining optimism and inspiring others, especially when faced with seemingly insurmountable odds.

The book will reveal how the simple act of listening—truly listening—can unlock doors you never knew existed, in both your personal and professional lives. You'll learn how small, daily victories can compound into life-changing achievements, and how serving others often leads to your own greatest successes.

We'll explore strategies for finding clarity and purpose amid life's inevitable chaos, and for building relationships that stand the test of time. You'll gain insights into how to continually push your boundaries, growing and evolving long after others might have settled.

The chapters will guide you through the nuances of mentorship—both as a mentee and as a mentor—showing how this reciprocal relationship can create ripples of positive change far beyond your immediate circle. Ultimately, we'll tackle the big questions of legacy, purpose, and fulfillment, providing you with tools not just to navigate life but to live it with intention and impact.

Through these lessons, drawn from decades of experience across various fields, you'll gain practical wisdom to help you navigate your own journey, overcome obstacles, build meaningful connections, and achieve success as you define it. This book offers insights applicable at any stage of life, helping you align your actions with your deepest values and aspirations.

This is the invitation I extend to you: to join me in grappling with the big questions and exploring answers through the stories and wisdom of the many teachers and mentors I have met, both in real life and in the pages of books. I can't tell you where your path will lead, but I can tell you it begins by asking . . .

What was I made for?

Turn the page, and let's find out together.

What You're Made For

To Be
a Trailblazer

Faith is taking the first step even
when you don't see the whole staircase.

—MARTIN LUTHER KING JR.

After my mom was institutionalized, nobody knew what to do with me.

My grandma—as I said, we called her "Dear"—had five jobs at the time, and one of them was working for this white family in Georgetown. She cleaned the house, made meals, baked, and all that stuff. One day Dear told the lady of the house about my mom and how she was trying to figure out what to do.

"Maybe Catherine can help," the woman suggested.

Catherine, it turned out, was the head of one of the branches of Catholic Charities. She was able to get Catholic Charities to pay to send me to a boarding school in Pennsylvania. It was a school for boys from broken homes called St. Michael's.

St. Michael's was founded in 1916 by Bishop Michael J. Hoban. He wanted to do more than feed and house boys without homes; he wanted to educate them and teach them practical skills they could use to make a living.

The boarding school sat on four hundred acres. Surrounded by woods and fields, it was the opposite of urban D.C. in every way, and there was plenty to do. When I woke up in the morning, it wasn't the clanging of street cars or vendors I heard, it was roosters. Here, the nuns and priests did the teaching and the students did the chores. I cleaned coops, baled hay, picked apples, scrubbed floors. I did whatever they asked me. I was just happy to be somewhere other than that little apartment.

Why did they pick me out of all the charity cases? I'll never know. Maybe they saw something in me. Maybe it was just luck, just a random act of kindness. In life, it doesn't really matter *why* you get an opportunity, only what you do with it.

I decided I wouldn't let this one pass me by.

It was here that I met Jerome Nadine, who would become a pivotal figure in my life. He was a trailblazer. He had been at St. Michael's before me, and as a Black student and basketball player, he had paved the way for someone like me. And after his time at the school, he'd been called to the priesthood, but his success and achievements in sports gave him credibility, and he used that to advocate for me.

Jerome kept pushing me to play basketball, mainly because I was so tall and a decent athlete. The basketball team, Father Nadine told me, travels all over the state to play games. I was looking for a way to occasionally get off campus for a little while and see the wider world, so I started wanting to play basketball. But I wasn't any good. Miraculously, I made the varsity team as a freshman. Years later, I found out that Jerome went to the basketball coach, Gene Villa, and said, "Hey, I think George is going to be really a good basketball player. Don't cut him. Keep him on the team. He's not ready right now, but keep him on the team."

How did he know? Again, what did he see in me? I have no idea, but to that request I owe the rest of my life. Gene promised to keep me on the team, and each year I got better and better.

But basketball was just part of the story. At St. Michael's, I found myself surrounded by a group of nuns who invested an enormous amount of time in me as a person and a student. Most of them couldn't tell you the rules of basketball, but they saw potential in me and set about helping me realize something I didn't even know existed.

There was one nun in particular, Sister Delora, who took a special interest in my basketball development. She'd get the keys to the gym, come and get me, and I'd shoot for an hour under her watchful eye. It was through the dedication of people like Sister Delora and Father Nadine that I began to believe I could become something.

It was also at St. Michael's that I converted to Catholicism, and Jerome became my godfather. This wasn't just a formal title; it represented a deep spiritual and personal connection that would last a lifetime. Father Nadine went on to serve as a chaplain at various military institutions. I visited him in San Diego a couple of months before he passed away, a final meeting with the man who had been such a crucial part of my journey. You don't have to believe in God, but there is such thing as angels in this world—people like Father Nadine are the real thing.

By my senior year, all this support and hard work paid off. I became the leading scorer in the state, somewhat of a spectacle. People filled the gym to watch me play, and college coaches started to take notice. After a game in which I scored thirty points and something like twenty rebounds against St. Rose of Carbondale, I walked out of the locker room, and as I was walking to the team bus, I heard someone say, "George!"

"Yes, sir," I said.

"My name is Jack Ramsay," he said, handing me his card. "I'm the head coach at Saint Joe's College in Philadelphia. We've been following you. We're planning to offer you a scholarship, and I just wanted to introduce myself because you're going to see me at a lot of games this season."

He shook my hand and told me, "Keep playing good." I'll never forget that. It was so simple: *Keep playing good.*

Simple isn't the same as easy, but it was worthy of a motto, one I would try to follow the rest of my life.

When I got on the bus, my coach asked me who I was talking to. I handed him the card, and once he looked at the name, immediately, my coach's demeanor changed.

"What did he say to you?" my coach asked.

"He said he's been watching me play and he's going to offer me a scholarship," I said.

Coach gave me a knowing nod and I had the sense that he was proud of me.

So I said, "Coach, let me ask you something."

"Sure," he said.

"What's a scholarship?"

I had no idea. I had no idea that a school would pay for your education, and in return, you play on their basketball team.

I was pretty excited to tell Dear, and I assumed she'd be excited and proud. It turns out, she was even more in the dark than I'd been. "I thought I raised you better than that," she said after I gave her the news.

"What do you mean?" I said. "I think you've done a great job in raising me." She had. There wasn't a day that went by that I hadn't done my best to live up to her example and tried to follow what she had taught me.

"Well, I'm disappointed in myself because I can't believe that you're naive enough to think that some white people are gonna pay for you to go to college just so you can play basketball," she told me. "It makes no sense. They're tricking you."

I couldn't help but laugh, but I also understood her skepticism. Given what she had experienced, Dear had every reason to be wary. Her reaction was a powerful reminder of how our past experiences can shape—and sometimes limit—our perception of future opportunities.

In many ways, Dear was a product of her history. She had survived hard years without experiencing much generosity or selflessness from white people. Even though my schooling up to that point had already been taken care of by a charity, it just didn't make sense to her that *sports* could be a way into higher education, let alone a free one!

Civil rights activist and author James Baldwin would talk about how we carry history with us; in fact, we're unconsciously controlled by it. Dear's reaction was a living example of this truth. Her history—our history—was present in that moment, shaping her interpretation of what seemed to me like an incredible opportunity. It was just beyond her comprehension—and to be honest, it was barely within mine. The idea that playing a game could open the door to a college education seemed almost too good to be true. But sometimes, the path forward requires us to see beyond the limitations of our past experiences, to imagine possibilities that our history might tell us are impossible.

Fortunately, the nuns were able to explain that this wasn't, in fact, too good to be true and that it was the opportunity of a lifetime, a path to a better future. Their perspective, less burdened by the specific history that shaped Dear's view, allowed them to see the scholarship for what it was: a chance for me to blaze a trail that neither Dear nor I had known existed.

They started making me stay after school every day to work on my studies. I didn't know it, but they were preparing me for the college entrance exams. Back then, each college had their own entrance exam. During a visit to Villanova, the head coach, Al Severance, said he was thinking about offering me a scholarship too, but first, I needed to take the entrance exam.

Needless to say, my early education in D.C. had not been great—"separate but equal" had always been a heinous lie—but through the grace of God and the grace of those dedicated nuns, I was able to make up for lost time. I ended up scoring so high, coach Severance offered me a scholarship on the spot. We called one of the nuns, Sister Evelina, to make sure that she approved of Villanova. She did, of course, because Villanova is a Catholic school. The next day, I accepted the scholarship to attend the university.

Like my transition from New Jersey and Florida Avenues to St. Michael's in Pennsylvania, when I got to Villanova, I was once again thrust into a world I knew very little about. I don't think I realized I was poor until I got to Villanova. I had hardly ever heard anyone talk about race until I got to Villanova.

It's important to understand the context of the time. I arrived at the university in the late 1950s, just a few years after the landmark 1954 Supreme Court ruling in *Brown v. Board of Education* had declared racial segregation in public schools unconstitutional. The country was still grappling with desegregation, and many institutions, particularly in the South, were resisting these changes. The riots that preceded James Meredith's enrollment at the University of Mississippi were still years away.

Villanova, a private Catholic university, was relatively progressive for its time, guided by its Augustinian values of social justice and inclusion. But that didn't mean it was easy being one of the very few Black students on campus. In 1959, Villanova's student enrollment was approximately three thousand. The exact number of Black students wasn't well documented, but it was likely in the single or low double digits.

Suddenly, I found myself in a sea of faces that didn't look like mine, navigating a world of privilege and opportunity that I had never experienced before. It was a stark contrast to my life in Washington, D.C., and even to St. Michael's, where at least there had been a handful of other Black students.

This transition wasn't just about academics or basketball. It was about learning to succeed in a world that was still in the early stages of integration, where my presence was both novel and, to some, challenging. The weight of being one of the few Black students on campus wasn't just a social burden; it was an intellectual one. I felt the pressure to represent my community, to excel not just for myself but for those who had never been given the chance. It was a constant balancing act—navigating the academic challenges while also confronting the subtle and overt racism that permeated every aspect of life. I was not just a student or an athlete. I was, whether I liked it or not, a pioneer.

This idea of forging your own path, of being a trailblazer, is beautifully illustrated in an old Arthurian legend, *La Queste del Saint Graal*, written by an anonymous monk in the thirteenth century. In the story, the knights of the Round Table are inspired to seek the Holy Grail after it briefly appears before them. But instead of setting out together, they make a profound choice. As the text reads, "They thought it would be a disgrace to go forth in a group. Each entered the Forest Adventurous at that point which he himself had chosen, where it was darkest and there was no way or path."

The renowned mythologist Joseph Campbell often cited this tale as a powerful metaphor for the individual's journey through life. To Campbell, it captured the essence of having the courage to follow your own path and find what truly fulfills you. "Where there's a way or a path," Campbell writes, "it is someone else's path."

What Campbell means here is profound: The well-trodden paths in life—the ones that are clear and easy to follow—have already been carved out by others. These paths represent conventional wisdom, societal expectations, or traditional routes to success. But true fulfillment, Campbell suggests, comes from forging your own way.

This doesn't mean that every individual has a predetermined, unique path waiting for them. Rather, it's an encouragement to venture into the unknown, to make choices based on your own values and aspirations rather than simply following in others' footsteps. It's about having the courage to step off the beaten track and create your own journey, even if that means facing uncertainty and challenges.

This ancient story resonates deeply with what it means to be a trailblazer. Just as each knight chose to enter the forest at its darkest point, where no path existed, I found myself venturing into unknown territory at Villanova. The campus was my Forest Adventurous, full of challenges and opportunities that I had to navigate on my own.

This is what an adventurous life is defined by—new environments, new groups, new cultures, new practices. Life as you know it is the work of men and women throughout history who had the courage and determination to blaze new trails forward.

And, of course, we're all pioneers of sorts, roaming into new frontiers of experience and opportunity. We're all put in front of paths never before traveled. Everyone has to be the pioneer, the first explorer, in their own story.

This is not easy. It is easy to default to a well-worn path. To fall in line behind what everyone else is doing, saying, and thinking.

Being a trailblazer is difficult. It's the road less traveled for a reason. It's filled with doubt, discomfort, detours, and dead ends. Lined with naysayers, puzzled looks, and unsolicited advice from those stuck on the beaten path. And only scattered with subtle signs that you're on the right path.

"It will be hard," Baldwin would write to his nephew. "You come from sturdy peasant stock, men who picked cotton and dammed rivers and built railroads, and, in the teeth of the most terrifying odds, achieved an unassailable and monumental dignity. You come from a long line of great poets, some of the greatest poets since Homer. One of them said, 'The very time I thought I was lost, My dungeon shook and my chains fell off.'"

I had to adapt and change, nowhere more than on the basketball court, where I was quickly confronted with the fact that I wasn't as good as I thought. I was no longer the biggest guy on the court. I could no longer rely on my size to score like I did in high school. To earn a starting spot, I needed to find a way to stand out, a path to getting some playing time.

I started to look around at my teammates. I looked at what the starters excelled at. I looked at what areas of the game guys focused on improving. We had great shooters and great passers. We had guys who stayed after practice to work on their ball handling. In practice, we spent a lot of time on defensive schemes. But nobody seemed to be a great rebounder. No one was staying after practice to work on their rebounding. No practice ever included a rebounding drill.

So I decided to become a rebounding specialist. If I got great at rebounding, I thought, the coaches would play me. There's no way that they're not going to play a guy who secures more possessions for the team. And, of course, my shooting, ball handling, passing, and defending would continue to improve through the work of typical practices. So if nothing else, I'd be a more well-rounded player.

I started staying after practice just to work on rebounding. In many ways, this approach to finding a unique path wasn't just about basketball; it was about life. It was about understanding that true success doesn't come from following the crowd, but from daring to be different, to see opportunities where others see obstacles. It was a lesson that would serve me well beyond the court.

I created drills to improve my reaction time, footwork, and body positioning. By my senior year, I had developed ten daily drills to refine my skills. I studied film to recognize patterns of rebound trajectories based on shot distance. In the weight room, I focused on things that would help me jump higher and exercises that would strengthen my lower body so that I was immovable under the basket.

Pretty soon, I was the rebounding guy. Coach once saw me doing one of my drills and asked, "Who showed you that?" Nobody. I made it up. It gave me a little bit of status among my teammates because I was the best at something. And the work paid off on the court. I went on to set single-game and season rebounding records in my time at Villanova, still eleventh on the all-time list.

At the time, I wouldn't have thought of it as a strategy, but that's exactly what it was. And it's a strategy that works in any field: find something that's underappreciated, not being addressed, or being overlooked, and get really good at it.

This philosophy of finding your niche and excelling in it reminds me of a poem I've always loved, "Be the Best of Whatever You Are," by Douglas Malloch. It speaks to the heart of what it means to be a trailblazer:

If you can't be the sun be a star;
. . . .
Be the best of whatever you are!

These lines encapsulate a profound truth: Success isn't about comparing yourself to others or trying to be something you're not. It's about finding your unique path, your special contribution, and giving it your all. Whether you're blazing a new trail or illuminating the way as a guiding star, what matters is that you're doing it to the best of your ability.

Later, when I got into coaching, the legendary Bob Knight gave me this advice: "George," he said, "if you're going to survive in this profession, you have to become the foremost expert in some phase of the game." When people early in their careers come to me for advice, I often tell them something similar: Be a trailblazer.

Find an untrodden path and blaze a trail. Find a void and fill it. Find a critical skill or area that most people are overlooking and become the foremost expert.

Whatever it is—a skill, a service, a demographic that's underserved, a phase of the game that's overlooked—if you become the foremost expert at something, you make yourself indispensable. You set yourself up not just for personal success but also for creating new possibilities for those who come behind you. For the kind of pioneering impact that can change another person's life, an industry, or even the world.

But this is not just a strategy for professional success. It's a fundamental aspect of being part of the human race. Where would we be if Harriet Tubman hadn't forged a path to freedom for hundreds of enslaved people through the Underground Railroad when most saw no way out? If Rosa Parks hadn't sparked the Montgomery bus boycott and Civil Rights Movement by refusing to give up her seat, courageously defying unjust segregation laws? If Mahatma Gandhi hadn't led the nonviolent resistance movement against British colonial rule in India, inspiring millions to fight for independence peacefully?

Being a trailblazer often means venturing into the unknown, where the way forward isn't always clear. You'll encounter dead ends, false starts, and paths that seem promising but ultimately lead nowhere. This is all part of the journey. Each setback and wrong turn is not a failure, but a lesson that brings you closer to finding your true path. The key is to keep moving, keep exploring, and to learn from every experience along the way.

While your specific path will feel at times like a deserted wilderness, you have plenty of company. Take heart: You are not alone. The pioneers, the innovators, the outcasts, the people who dared to be the first, to break from convention, to hope and dream of a better future and beat down the path to get there—it is a long and profound lineage of trailblazers you are joining.

So, yes, know that it won't be an easy path.

But also keep in mind that it will be uniquely yours.

That with each step, you take your place in the long line of trailblazers who have paved the path of history.

That you come from sturdy trailblazer stock.

That you were made to be a trailblazer.

To Listen
and Learn

When you talk, you are only repeating what you already
know. But if you listen, you may learn something new.

—DALAI LAMA

As a young boy growing up in the 1940s, I spent countless
hours at the feet of wise women. In those days, the well-
worn adage was that children were to be seen and not
heard. So when Dear, who raised me, would bring me along on
visits to "my lady friends," as she would say, I sat quietly as the
neighborhood ladies gossiped, swapped stories, and dissected the
latest church sermon.

At first, I didn't pay close attention. But these outings weren't
just social calls, and I wasn't just a tagalong. Grandma had a reason for her going and me being there. On the walk home, she
would quiz me: "George, what's something Miss Jenkins said that
you found interesting?" "Did you learn anything from Miss Sim-
mons's story about her son?"

She was turning on my young ears. In her gentle yet deliberate
way, she was revising that old adage, making sure that I not only

saw but heard the ladies. Her concern wasn't that I was silent and invisible. It was that I was present, attentive, and ready to catch the nuggets of wisdom that the ladies were dropping. And it was that I was taught that listening is an active, not a passive, act. "The best way to participate in a conversation," she would say, "is by listening."

Looking back, I realize now that my grandmother and her friends were my first audiobook. She didn't just bring me along to listen; she curated experiences and conversations that would shape my understanding of the world. Through her, I learned not just facts and stories, but how to learn, how to listen actively, and how to distill wisdom from everyday conversations.

Maya Angelou, who was born a few years before I was, talked about feeling like "a giant ear" in her childhood. She didn't talk much, but she *listened*. She loved *voices*. She absorbed everything around her, trying to make sense of the incomprehensible world.

I learned that there was a time to listen and a time to speak. I learned to pocket a few questions and takeaways for those walks home. Initially, it was mostly a passive act—it was because I knew Grandma was going to quiz me, and I wanted to make sure I was ready. But soon, it became active—it was because I knew there was a nugget of wisdom in something Miss Jenkins said, and I wanted to make sure I caught it correctly.

I began to look for any opportunity to listen and learn. At home, we couldn't afford a TV, but we got a radio when I was eleven years old. The family would huddle around for Friday Night Fights, listening intently as the announcer described the jabs, hooks, and uppercuts thrown by boxing legends like Joe Louis, Rocky Marciano, and Sugar Ray Robinson. We'd gather for the latest *Amos 'n' Andy* episodes, laughing along with the antics and adventures of the comedy duo. There were news broadcasts, game shows, soap operas, detective thrillers, gospel hymns, live church sermons, weather forecasts, interviews, and educational programs.

In every case, you had to listen closely. To follow the action in the boxing ring, to get the joke, the plot twists, or the insights in a sermon, you couldn't let your mind wander. You had to be fully present, fully engaged, fully attuned to the subtle details and layers beneath the surface of words—a skill that extends far beyond the living room.

This early training in active listening served me well throughout my life, but it wasn't until I got to college that I truly began to appreciate its value. At Villanova, I found myself surrounded by people who had so much to teach me—if only I was willing to listen. The nuns who had invested so much time in me at St. Michael's had prepared me well for this. They had instilled in me a hunger for knowledge and a respect for wisdom, regardless of its source.

My coaches too became invaluable sources of learning. Coach Al Severance, who had offered me the scholarship, was a wealth of basketball knowledge. But more than that, he taught me about life, about perseverance, about rising to challenges. I made it a point to absorb everything I could from him, not just his words, but his actions, his decisions, the way he carried himself.

Even my teammates became my teachers. Coming from a different background, many of them had experiences and perspectives that were entirely new to me. By listening to their stories, their jokes, their concerns, I began to understand the wider world in ways I never had before.

But perhaps one of my greatest teachers came from outside the college environment. I first met Wilt Chamberlain when he was a senior at Overbrook High School in West Philadelphia. At that time, Overbrook was the basketball school in the city, mainly because of Wilt. I was older, in college, but we met on the playgrounds, and we just clicked. We'd sit on the sidelines, waiting for the next game, talking about basketball, life, whatever came to mind. One day, Wilt picked me for his team because he knew I had led the country in rebounding in college. That's how our friendship started.

Little did I know that this connection would lead to one of the most enlightening summers of my young life. One day, I went over to Wilt's house, and we were heading up to the playground together. On the way, he told me he was getting a lot of requests to speak at kids' camps in the Catskill Mountains during the summer. Then, he surprised me by saying, "I'll hire you to be my chauffeur. I'll pay you a hundred dollars a day." I agreed right away. Wilt had this purple Bentley convertible, so I'd drive him around the mountains to these different children's camps. These weren't basketball camps; they were just regular camps, mostly attended by kids from Jewish families.

At first, we'd just put on a show, doing all kinds of dunks, and we'd take pictures with the kids. But as I observed and listened to the interactions, I saw an opportunity to add more value. I suggested we create a little more structure, like a short lecture on offense and defense. Wilt liked the idea, so we incorporated that into our routine. This experience taught me the value of not just participating, but actively seeking ways to improve and add depth to any situation.

Spending so much time with Wilt that summer, I learned more than just basketball skills. There is something about champions that is just *different*. How they carry themselves. What they notice. What they expect. What they think is possible.

I observed his dedication to his craft, his interactions with fans, and his approach to his growing fame. Wilt wasn't just a basketball player; he was an all-around athlete. He ran on the mile relay team at the University of Kansas, he high-jumped, and he even started a pro volleyball team. People didn't believe me when I said that, but it was true. Watching Wilt, I learned the importance of versatility and pushing beyond perceived limitations.

Perhaps the most striking lesson came from observing the stark difference between Wilt's approach to the game and my own. Wilt had this incredible drive to dominate every time he played. For him, it wasn't just about winning; it was about embarrassing his opponents. He had a hunger for perfection and greatness, and he held himself to the highest standards. This killer instinct, shared by players like Michael Jordan, was something you couldn't teach. It was just in them.

I knew at some level that I just didn't have that.

I was smart enough to know that if I ever played against them, I had to be careful. After the game, we'd go out for pizza or a beer, but on the court, I knew better than to try and guard either one of them. This taught me a valuable lesson about recognizing and respecting different approaches to excellence, even if they differed from my own.

In those days, scouting other teams was difficult. Unlike today, where coaches and players can access detailed game footage, statistical analyses, and advanced scouting reports with ease, the methods of scouting back then were rudimentary and relied heavily on word of mouth and personal observation.

As a player at Villanova, when our coach would verbally share whatever he knew about an upcoming opponent, it was like I was back at Miss Jenkins's or on the floor next to the radio. Within the coach's words, I knew, were insights that could make the difference between me having a good game and a bad game, between the team winning and losing, between success and failure.

Later, when I became a coach, I made it a point to ensure my players knew I wanted to hear their observations and insights. During time-outs, I would often ask, "What are you seeing out there?" I asked that constantly. It gives the player the sense that they have a stake in the team's strategy and decision-making process, which sends a powerful message about their value and role on the team. But it also gives the coach information that is hard to get otherwise. The subtleties in the opponents' schemes, adjustments, player tendencies—critical insights like these can often be obvious on the court but hard to perceive from the sidelines.

Of course, I wouldn't blindly act on every piece of information shared. Sometimes, a player's observation can be something that shifts the game plan and turns the tide of the game. But other times, it can be something that does not consider broader tactical implications, is colored by their emotions, or applies only within their specific individual matchup. The good coach, just like the good listener, filters the information and catches only the most relevant and actionable insights.

This ability to filter, to discern, to sift the signal from the noise—I got to witness this skill at the highest level through working with Nike cofounder Phil Knight, a true master of the art.

I remember one particular meeting that was true to form, perfectly illustrating Knight's ability to cut through clutter and get straight to the core of an issue or idea. Our marketing team had prepared an extensive and elaborate presentation to address declining sales in one of our basketball product lines. The room was filled with detailed charts, sophisticated financial projections, and complex strategies. With a flair of fancy jargon, the team presented a meticulously crafted narrative that danced around the supposed need for a significant financial injection. Knight listened silently, intently, patiently, with an unvarying facial expression that made it impossible to tell if he was impressed, confused, bored, excited, or annoyed.

When the team finally finished the presentation, Knight leaned back in his chair, still without giving away any hint of his thoughts or feelings, then said, "Throwing money at a problem is rarely the solution."

I'll never forget him saying that: *Throwing money at a problem is rarely the solution.* Nine words that got straight to the bottom of layers and layers of complexity. That carried more weight and wisdom than a hundred presentation slides or a thousand data points. It didn't dismiss the team's hard work or the complexity of the issue at hand, but instead urged them to go deeper, to dive beneath their surface understanding of the problem, and to think more creatively about potential solutions.

In today's world, the art of listening seems to be under threat. Social media has trained us to believe that what matters most is what we have to say. We're talking more than ever, broadcasting our thoughts to the world with every post, tweet, and status update. But in this cacophony of voices, it often seems like nobody is truly hearing each other.

We've become so focused on crafting our next response, our next witty comment, that we've forgotten how to listen. We skim, we scan, we scroll, but we rarely stop to absorb and consider what others are saying. We're more connected than ever, yet in many ways, we're more isolated, trapped in echo chambers of our own making.

This is why the skill of listening—real, active, engaged listening—is more crucial than ever. It's a skill that can set you apart in a world where everyone is clamoring to be heard. It's a skill that can open doors, build relationships, and lead to insights and opportunities that you might otherwise miss.

Today, at eighty-seven, I'm still working to sharpen my listening skills. Before I walk into any meeting, I write down at the top of my notepad a ratio for how much I want to talk versus listen (talk 20 percent, listen 80 percent). You'd think I'd have it down by this point in my life, but no, it's still a struggle and a matter of discipline. If I think of a question or a comment, instead of interrupting, I write it down, pocketing it just like I would when I was to be seen and not heard by Grandma and her ladies.

I make sure to keep myself around people I want to listen to and learn from, and I make sure to ask them, just as I used to ask my players, "What are you seeing out there?" "What are you hearing?" "What's been interesting to you lately?" "Read anything good recently?"

In this age of information overload, I've found that these simple questions can lead to the most enlightening conversations. They cut through the noise and get to the heart of what people are truly thinking and experiencing.

In my journey, I've come to embrace a truth that Ralph Waldo Emerson once expressed: everyone is better than us at something—even if it's a little thing. If we want to keep growing and improving, we should focus on finding and learning from these strengths in others. This mindset turns every interaction into an opportunity for growth.

And after a day full of listening, I review my notes and try to distill what I've learned into nuggets of wisdom, core insights, pithy Knight-like one-liners. This practice of reflection is crucial. It's not enough to just hear words; we need to process them, to let them sink in, to consider how they apply to our lives and our understanding of the world.

In a world that seems to value noise over substance, where the loudest voice often gets the most attention, I believe we need to rediscover the power of listening. We need to remember that wisdom often comes in whispers, not shouts. That the most profound insights often come from unexpected sources. That sometimes, the most important thing we can say is nothing at all.

We have two ears and one mouth.

We were made to talk less than we listen.

We were made to participate in conversations mostly by listening.

We were made to listen and learn.

And in doing so, we open ourselves up to a world of wisdom, understanding, and connection that we might otherwise miss. In a world that's constantly telling us to speak up, to stand out, to make ourselves heard, perhaps the most revolutionary act is to be quiet, to listen, and to learn.

To Seek
Out Wisdom

Wisdom is not a product of schooling but
of the lifelong attempt to acquire it.

—ALBERT EINSTEIN

I n life, wisdom rarely falls into our laps. Unlike the apples in
Newton's apocryphal story, it rarely bonks us on the head
while we're resting in the shade. It's not something we stumble
upon by chance while going about our daily routines. It doesn't
automatically come with age, education, or position.

No, wisdom demands that we seek it out. It requires effort,
curiosity, and a willingness to step out of our comfort zones, to
engage deeply with new ideas, and to actively pursue knowledge
from a variety of sources. Wisdom isn't something handed down
by institutions or represented by degrees—it's earned through exploration, reflection, and a relentless openness to learning from
the world around us.

A few years ago, I was reading a book when the word *mastermind* caught my eye. I'd never heard that term. As was my habit,
I circled it and made a note to look it up later. When I dove into

researching the concept online, I was fascinated by what I found—the idea of a group of like-minded individuals coming together to share knowledge, challenge each other, and accelerate their personal and professional growth. Among other things, I came across an article about an event called Mastermind Dinners, which I shared with a few friends.

Wisdom, like life, is a team sport. It turns out, one of the friends I had sent the article to had attended one of those dinners and offered to connect me. "Go for it!" I replied back over email.

I soon found myself with an invitation to a conference in Ojai, California, and what turned out to be a wonderful and transformative experience. At eighty-three!

I've been to countless events in my life, but there at the Ojai Valley Inn, I was overwhelmed.

Every night, I went to bed with a headache—not from stress or frustration, but from the sheer volume of new information crammed into my brain. It was exhilarating. I took at least fifty pages of notes each day, staying up until midnight just to capture all the insights and ideas swirling in my head.

But it wasn't just about the information. It was about the people and the new ways of thinking and being they introduced me to. The mastermind event was a melting pot of minds from all walks of life. There were tech entrepreneurs fresh from Silicon Valley, entertainment moguls from Hollywood, seasoned executives from Wall Street, and everything in between. The age range spanned from ambitious twentysomethings to wise octogenarians. Some had come from humble beginnings, others from privilege, but all were there with the same purpose: to learn and grow.

What struck me most was how this diverse group was unified by an insatiable curiosity and drive to seek out wisdom. Here I was, a former basketball coach from another era, rubbing shoulders with young tech wizards and veteran CEOs alike. The conversations were electric, jumping from topics like artificial intelligence to ancient philosophy, from the latest business trends to timeless life lessons.

I vividly remember sitting at a lunch table with about eight or nine people—a young app developer, a bestselling author, a retired general, and a cutting-edge scientist among them. Despite our vastly different backgrounds, we found common ground in our hunger for knowledge. They peppered me with questions about my experiences in sports and civil rights, while I eagerly soaked up their insights on technology and current global trends.

It struck me as I was sitting there that this idea of a "mastermind" was not as unfamiliar to me as I had once thought. I was reminded of my time with the Black Coaches Association (BCA), an organization a few of us founded in 1988 in the wake of Proposition 42, an NCAA ruling that denied athletic scholarships to freshmen who didn't meet certain academic criteria. The policy disproportionately affected Black athletes from underprivileged backgrounds, preventing them from playing sports even if they were qualified. Many of us saw it as a thinly veiled attempt to limit opportunities for young Black men, who we knew were deserving of an education and we knew we could help.

What I found curious was that people would frequently ask, "Well, why do you have to have a Black Coaches Association?" In fact, it was one of the differences of opinion Bob Knight and I had. Around the time we started the BCA, Bob said to me, "George, help me understand. What is the necessity for a Black Coaches Association? Why do you need a Black Coaches Association? We don't have a White Coaches Association. We don't have a Puerto Rican Coaches Association. We don't have an Italian Coaches Association." And I said, "Bob, do me a favor. I'm not going to answer that question until you think about it for a week. And if you still don't understand, come back and we'll talk about it." He never said another word to me about it.

Anyone who takes a close look at America can see that, more than any other nation, it's built on special interest groups. The Black Coaches Association was no different than the movements for women's rights, religious rights, or LGBTQ+ rights. Special interest groups are born from frustration—when voices go unheard, they band together to amplify their message.

The BCA wasn't just a group fighting against discrimination—it was a community of like-minded individuals who came together to share ideas, support each other, and amplify our voices. I remember appearing on *Charlie Rose* alongside John Chaney, Nolan Richardson, and Rudy Washington. We took our fight to Capitol Hill, met with the Congressional Black Caucus, and challenged the NCAA's discriminatory policies. Just like in a mastermind, we recognized that even though we were technically competitors—each leading different teams, fighting for the same small number of jobs and endorsements—we were stronger together. Our unity became our greatest weapon, and it allowed us to effect real, lasting change.

The idea is that even competitors can help each other. Because in the end, we are not so much competing against each other as we are trying to beat the odds, trying to wrest something away from powerful interests, trying to make the world better.

Although our association back in the 1980s and '90s was in part based on our identities, one of the things I appreciated most about this recent event was the diversity of thought it brought together. If you're in an environment where everyone thinks just like you, it can get really boring really fast. But at the mastermind event, every conversation was an opportunity to step into a new world, to see things from a completely different perspective. It reinforced something I've always believed: wisdom doesn't always come to you—you have to seek it out, sometimes in the most unlikely of places.

I recall thinking to myself, "This is what growth looks like." It's not about surrounding yourself with people who think exactly like you do. It's about seeking out those who can challenge your assumptions, expand your horizons, and push you to think in new ways. It's about putting yourself in situations where you're not the most knowledgeable person in the room, where you can discover wisdom you never knew existed.

One evening, I found myself in a deep discussion with a young entrepreneur about the parallels between building a successful team in sports and in business. Despite our age difference and disparate fields, we found so many common principles that we could both learn from and apply in our respective areas.

This experience reinforced another belief I've long held: if you and I agree on everything, one of us is unnecessary. The real value comes from diversity—not just in terms of race or gender, but in experiences, in ways of thinking, in approaches to problem-solving. But this value is only realized if we actively seek it out, if we deliberately put ourselves in the path of new and challenging ideas.

The mastermind event wasn't just about networking. It was about creating a space where wisdom could flow freely, where each person's unique experiences and insights contributed to a greater pool of knowledge that we could all draw from. It was a vivid reminder that wisdom doesn't discriminate—it can come from the youngest start-up founder or the most seasoned industry veteran. The key is to remain open, curious, and always ready to learn. And to recognize that while wisdom might sometimes fall into your lap, more often than not, you have to seek it out.

That mastermind event changed my life. It opened my eyes to how much there was still to learn, still to discover. I couldn't wait to get up each morning and start absorbing more. It was a moment when I realized there was so much more out there to learn that I didn't know, and I was mentally excited every day. It taught me that the pursuit of wisdom is an active endeavor, one that requires us to go out into the world and find it.

But here's the thing: you don't need to attend an exclusive event to have this kind of transformative experience. The great masterminds of all time are waiting for you in places that are much more accessible: your local bookstores and libraries. After all, it was in a book that I learned that term in the first place!

I go to bookstores six to eight times a week. There's a Barnes & Noble in El Segundo, California, where I stop every morning to pick up my newspapers—*The New York Times*, *The Wall Street Journal*, the *Los Angeles Times*, and the *Daily Breeze*. I also frequent the Barnes & Noble in Marina del Rey about five times a week. For a long time, there was an incredible Black-owned independent bookstore in the Leimert Park section of Los Angeles— *The New York Times* even recognized it as the number one bookstore in America. While it was in business, not a month went by that I didn't visit.

At each of these bookstores, I know every cashier, every manager, and where every book is located. They're like a second home to me. Walking through the aisles, greeting familiar faces, and losing myself in the pages of a good book are as much a part of my daily routine as anything else. These places aren't just stores—they're sanctuaries, where I connect with the wisdom of the world and the people who help make it accessible. And they remind me that wisdom can be found anywhere—sometimes you just have to go looking for it.

In her book about the 1986 Los Angeles Public Library fire, Susan Orlean beautifully captures what these places mean: "A library is a good place to soften solitude; a place where you feel part of a conversation that has gone on for hundreds and hundreds of years even when you're all alone. The library is a whispering post. You don't need to take a book off a shelf to know there is a voice inside that is waiting to speak to you, and behind that was someone who truly believed that if he or she spoke, someone would listen."

Books, in this way, are wonderful friends. They are always there. They speak wisdom, but offer their advice quietly. They have an unlimited capacity for listening. They offer so much and ask for essentially nothing in return. But they won't come to you—you have to go out and find them, open their pages, and let their wisdom into your life.

I've always believed in what I call the Three Wise Men theory: always come bearing gifts. And my gifts are always books.

I learned this lesson early, studying the story of the three wise men who brought gifts to the newborn Jesus. I decided that whenever I go somewhere, I should come bearing gifts too. And what better gift than the gift of knowledge?

Over the years, people have told me that the books I've given them have changed their lives. It's incredibly rewarding to know that by sharing a book, you're potentially opening up a whole new world for someone.

But I've also made an interesting observation about giving away books. If I notice that someone doesn't read the books I give them, I stop. To me, an unread book on a shelf is an assassination—it's the death of potential wisdom and growth. Why would I give someone a book I know they're not going to read when I could give it to somebody who will benefit from it, grow, and discover more about who they are?

In my house, much to my wife's dismay, we have a dedicated library with over twenty-five hundred books. I've even bought mobile book racks—the kind you find in libraries and bookstores—that hold seventy-five books each. I bought four of those because I had books stacked up on the floor and it was driving my wife nuts. Then there's my office, with probably another two hundred books on the shelves.

I have strategic reading points throughout the house too. On my side of the bed, I keep eight books and about four stenographer pads. Every night before bed, I spend at least thirty minutes reading.

So, whether it's at a mastermind event, in the aisles of your local bookstore, during quiet moments of reflection with a thought-provoking book, or when a word or idea catches your attention and prompts you to dive deeper into research, wisdom is out there waiting for you. All you have to do is seek it out. Just as we discussed the importance of being a trailblazer earlier, seeking out wisdom often requires us to venture into unfamiliar territory, to blaze new trails in our pursuit of knowledge.

Because that's what we're made for—to learn, to grow, to connect with the great minds of past and present through the written word. But don't wait for it to come to you—go out and find it. Wisdom is out there, waiting for those who seek it.

We are living in the greatest time in history right now. Every day, our lives are filled with insurmountable opportunities for personal growth. These opportunities are everywhere—we just need to reach out and embrace them, make them part of our lives. If you don't go to that event, you don't meet that person who becomes a lifelong friend. If you don't pick up that book, you miss out on knowledge that could change your life forever.

I've learned that being in environments where everyone thinks alike and agrees on everything stifles growth. Seek out diverse perspectives, challenge your assumptions, and never stop learning. And above all, actively seek out wisdom in all its forms—it won't always find you, but if you look, you'll find it.

We're made to seek out wisdom, wherever it may be found. Make it a priority.

Spend time each day between the pages of a good book and in the quiet corners of a library.

Go down rabbit holes.

Let your curiosity lead you from one discovery to the next. Look up words you don't know.

Share what you're learning with others—you never know what might come of it.

Build relationships with people who share your love of knowledge—booksellers, librarians, fellow readers, mentors, and curious minds.

Linger in the stacks.

Surround yourself with books.

Explore ideas relentlessly, and let your curiosity take you to places you never imagined.

Engage deeply with what you find, and watch as your world expands with each discovery.

Every day is an opportunity to expand your mind, challenge your beliefs, and grow in ways you never thought possible. Wisdom doesn't come to those who wait—it comes to those who actively pursue it, who immerse themselves in learning, and who engage with the world around them with curiosity and passion.

So go, seek wisdom, and embrace the journey of discovery—that's what you're made for.

To Struggle

One day, in retrospect, the years of
struggle will strike you as the most beautiful.

—SIGMUND FREUD

January 26, 1980. That date is etched in my memory forever. But to understand why, we need to go back a few years.

When I became the head coach at Washington State University in 1972, the Cougars hadn't beaten UCLA in over a decade. And in the twenty-three-season rivalry, we'd never won in Los Angeles. UCLA, under the legendary coach John Wooden, was the gold standard of college basketball, a dynasty that had steamrolled nearly every opponent that dared to challenge them. They had won seven national championships, six of which were consecutive, and recently finished their third undefeated season under Wooden.

My first game against UCLA as head coach was a brutal introduction to that reality. On February 10, 1973, we lost 88–50, to what some college basketball historians rate as the best team ever. They were an absolute juggernaut, loaded with six future NBA players. Bill Walton would go on to become one of the greatest centers in the history of the game. Jamaal Wilkes, a silky-smooth forward, would win multiple NBA championships. Swen Nater was a force in the paint, Greg Lee the brainy floor general, Dave Meyers a versatile forward, and Ralph Drollinger, towering at seven feet, two inches, dominated inside.

A week after that initial thrashing, we faced them again and lost 96–64. These two defeats were wins 63 and 66 in UCLA's legendary 88-game winning streak, the longest in men's college basketball history. The pattern continued. Year after year, we'd face UCLA, and year after year, we'd walk off the court defeated. Even as we improved as a team, as I grew as a coach, the result was always the same: another loss to UCLA.

At the time, each loss felt like a setback, a reminder of how far we still had to go. But looking back now, I realize those struggles were shaping us, preparing us for something greater. We were learning, growing, and building resilience with every defeat.

The hardest losses, the ones that truly stung, were those where victory was just within reach. In 1978, we traveled to Pauley Pavilion with a nine-game winning streak and a 10-2 record. UCLA was ranked fourth in the nation, and everyone expected us to lose like we always had in Los Angeles.

But that night was different. We played the game of our lives. We were leading 59–58 with 10 seconds left when Terry Clark stepped to the line for a one-and-one free throw. Clark was the number one foul shooter in the country. He made the first. As the ball passed through the net, I thought, We've done it. I felt the weight of those years of losses lift.

Then came the whistle.

Referee Tom Harrington called a lane violation on our center, Stuart House. The point was wiped off the board, and UCLA got the ball. In the final seconds, UCLA rushed down the court, and their All-American David Greenwood dunked the ball, just beating the buzzer.

Final score: UCLA 60, Washington State 59.

I was devastated. I later told reporters, "Even the Good Lord wouldn't convince me that game wasn't stolen from us." It felt like more than just a loss—it felt like an injustice. Like someone had it out for us.

It was after this game or another one—it's been almost fifty years—but I remember after a tough loss, John Wooden clasped my hand and told me, "I've seen a lot of basketball in my time, and I have to say, you guys should have won that game."

John Wooden told the truth. Even when it didn't favor him.

"But," he said, "there'll be better days ahead."

The truth again.

Those words echoed in my mind as we made the long trip back to Pullman, Washington, and they stayed with me in the years that followed. We faced UCLA again and again, each time coming up short, extending the streak to twenty-seven losses.

But I held on to Coach Wooden's words, believing that our time would come. Little did I know then how right he would be, or how those struggles were forging us into something stronger.

It came on January 26, 1980.

The sold-out crowd at Friel Court in Pullman was buzzing as Stuart House and UCLA's James Wilkes lined up for the opening tip. I had five seniors in my starting lineup—guys who had been through those bitter defeats and were hungry for redemption.

The game started slow, both teams feeling each other out. But as the minutes ticked by, I could see our confidence growing. Don Collins, our star player, was finding his rhythm. Terry Kelly was knocking down shots with the precision of a marksman. On defense, we were locked in—talking, switching, frustrating UCLA at every turn. Their rhythm was out of sync. Every time they tried to run a play, we were there to disrupt, to confuse, to remind them they were up against a veteran squad that knew how to battle.

I paced the sidelines, constantly talking to my guys. "Move your feet!" I'd shout to keep them sharp on defense. "Switch on the screen!" "Eyes up, Don! You've got space to drive!" Collins was in the zone, but I wanted him even more locked in. Terry Kelly had been deadly from the perimeter, but I kept reminding him, "Keep shooting, Terry—don't think, just shoot!"

I knew every possession was crucial. Against a team like UCLA, we couldn't afford a moment's lapse. Or a bad call—a clean steal in the post by Bryan Rison, plain as day, whistled as a foul. Rison was breaking away, all alone, what would have been an easy layup. Even the commentators were confused. Ross Porter, calling the game, initially thought the foul was in the backcourt, speculating if it was on Sanders or Holton, UCLA players. Then the realization hit. "Oh no, it's going the other way," Porter said, surprised. "They're going to call it on Rison. . . . George Raveling doesn't like the call either—he thought his player stole it cleanly."

I was livid. That should have been an easy two points, no question. I let the refs hear it, making it clear they owed us for that blown call. As UCLA inbounded the ball, we locked in on defense—tight, aggressive, giving them no space. A few tense moments later, we forced a three-second violation. It was exactly the response we needed. Rison took the ball down the court, driving hard to the basket. Just as he approached the paint, the UCLA defender poked it loose—but this time, the whistle blew in our favor. The ref called a foul on the defender. There it was—our makeup call.

The first half wore on, with neither team able to pull away. We never led by more than 7, and UCLA never held a lead at all. The score was tied at 2 early on, and they closed the gap to 16–15 midway through the half. Every possession felt like a battle, and I knew this game was going to be a grind until the final buzzer.

With 4:15 left in the first half, the ref on the far side of the play, close to where I was standing, blew his whistle to call traveling on a UCLA player. But the crowd was so loud that neither the players nor the other refs heard the whistle. Play continued for a few seconds, long enough for UCLA's Mike Sanders to go up for a dunk. One of our guards, Terry Kelly, planted his feet to take the charge, and one of the other refs called a blocking foul on Kelly.

"George Raveling comes out on the court," Porter called out on the broadcast, "at least fifteen feet out to argue the call."

I knew I didn't really need to storm out fifteen feet onto the court. The traveling call had been clear—I knew the refs would huddle up and get it right. So it was a low-stakes moment, and that's exactly why I seized it. I wasn't on the court to argue the call—I was there to fire up my guys. We were in a fight, and I knew if they saw me out there laying it all on the line, they'd get fired up to do the same.

And it worked. The refs sorted out the call, and we got the ball back. Then, we went on a tear. We surged ahead with an 11–1 run, taking a 12-point lead into halftime.

In the locker room, I gathered the team around. The energy was high, and we had to keep it that way. "Listen up, boys," I said. "Great start, but we know UCLA isn't going to roll over. They've got a legacy of comebacks, and we can't give them an inch. We haven't won anything yet."

As we came out for the second half, I knew we couldn't let up. Don Collins, riding the momentum from the first half, quickly added another basket, pushing our lead to 16 points. Our defense remained relentless, forcing UCLA into tough shots and turn-overs. With 15:46 left in the game, UCLA called a time-out. We were up by 20, a lead that even in my wildest dreams I hadn't imagined. As I huddled with the team, I emphasized the impor-tance of staying focused. "We've got them on the ropes," I said, "but we've got to keep going. Keep the pressure on." It had taken me fourteen tries to beat UCLA, and I wasn't about to get com-fortable now.

Our aggressive play paid off. At the 13-minute mark, we ex-tended our lead to 23 points, the largest of the game. I could feel the energy in the arena building. The crowd was behind us, louder than I'd ever heard in Pullman.

As the clock ticked down to 8:33, we were up by 21. I called a time-out, not to make adjustments, but to keep our guys focused. I could see the finish line, but I also knew how quickly things could change in basketball. This was UCLA—the team that had beaten us twenty-seven straight times. With 4:56 left and a 67–50 lead, I called another time-out. Some might have thought it un-necessary with a 17-point lead, but I wanted to tell my guys, "Don't let up! Finish strong!"

Even with 1:50 left and a 15-point lead, I was coaching as if it were a tie game. I remember calling a time-out and laying into the guys, demanding they play these final two minutes as if our lives depended on it.

With eight seconds left on the clock, we were up 78–64, and

the crowd could feel it. The students were chanting, "Na na na na, hey hey hey, goodbye."

Seven seconds, six—Terry Kelly steals the ball and throws it to Bryan Rison, who anticipated the play and is already streaking toward the basket.

Rison catches the ball in stride—four seconds, three—he takes a single step into the paint, rising for the layup—two seconds, one—he scores.

Washington State 80, UCLA 64.

The buzzer sounds, and as it does, I throw both arms in the air—higher than I think I've ever raised them in my life—and I keep them there, like I'm trying to hold on to this moment. I start walking toward the UCLA bench, but I can't help it—I look up at the rafters, spin around, still walking, hands still in the air.

I drop my arms just long enough to shake hands with their coaching staff, but the second those formalities are over, both arms shoot straight back up in the air.

Fans are swarming the court. I give one of them double high fives, then shake hands with another.

I feel a rush coming from behind—my guys, hugging me from all sides. Four of them at once. Then a fifth. A sixth and seventh. They're all around me, the momentum taking us off the court. Suddenly, I'm lifted into the air. They're carrying me—through the crowd and down the tunnel.

We did it. We finally did it. We beat UCLA.

But the most emotional moment was yet to come. In the locker room, we were all enjoying the win, appreciating the significance of what we'd done. Then Sam Jankovich, our athletic director, burst into the locker room. "George," he said, "you've got to come back out on the floor." I looked at him, confused. "For what?" I asked.

He smiled, almost giddy. "Everyone is still in their seats, they're chanting for you. They aren't leaving until you come back out."

I didn't believe him at first, but as I made my way back down the tunnel, I could hear it—the roar of the crowd chanting, "We want George! We want George!"

By the time I reached the floor, I had tears in my eyes. The arena was still packed, and when the crowd saw me, they erupted. The noise was deafening. I didn't know how to react. I just stood there, overwhelmed, as the chants kept coming, as if they could go on forever.

For those few minutes, I was completely overcome with emotion. It wasn't just the win. It was everything—the years of losses, the effort we had put in, the feeling that this victory was for all of us, for the players, for the fans, for the university. I broke down and cried, right there on the floor. It was the most emotional moment of my coaching career.

As I stood there, the crowd chanting my name, I didn't know what to say. But when the noise finally died down, I managed to find the words: "On behalf of the players, thanks to the students— I know you're in finals. It might have been twenty-seven games since we beat them, but when we did, it was a hell of a game." The crowd roared again, and all I could do was soak it in. I had never experienced anything like it. Later, I sent a letter to *The Evergreen*, the school newspaper, thanking the fans. I told them that while I was happy about the win, the most touching moment of my career came after the game when they called me back onto the court. That moment would go down as one of the most emotional times of my life. I was truly at a loss for words.

As I later reflected on the students and fans chanting and refusing to leave their seats, and my players deliriously celebrating, I realized that the significance of that win wasn't really about what had happened on the court that night. The game itself didn't have any of the typical elements of an all-time classic. No buzzer-beater. No dramatic comeback. No overtime or last-second heroics. In fact, we led comfortably for most of the second half.

The significance was created by everything that had led up to that night. Years of close calls, heartbreaks, and coming up short. It was the near misses, the bad calls, the long bus rides home after yet another loss that made that January 26, 1980, win unforgettable.

In that moment, I understood a profound truth: our struggles give meaning to our triumphs. We think we want things to go our way. We think we want to get our way immediately. We think we want things to be easy.

We are mistaken. "What man actually needs is not a tension-less state," Viktor Frankl explained, "but rather the striving and struggling for some goal worthy of him." It is not easy to reach your outer limits. It will challenge you. It will be painful. It may well break you.

Those years of losses, frustrating as they were, had made this victory sweeter than any easy win could have been. Each defeat had taught us something, had strengthened our resolve, had brought us closer as a team.

And this truth extends far beyond the basketball court. My life has been a series of struggles that deepened my appreciation for that moment in a way I wouldn't have known if my path had been easy or one of unearned privilege. The loss of my parents, growing up in a tough neighborhood, being sent to boarding school, and facing racial discrimination—all these hardships, when the weight of life made my shoulders slump—made the experience of raising both arms in victory that much more meaningful and beautiful.

Think about times in your own life—whether it's a job interview that didn't go as planned, a relationship that ended when you thought it would last, or a personal goal that seemed to slip just out of reach. Those moments hurt. They're frustrating. But in hindsight, it's often those experiences that shape us the most. Each failure forces you to reexamine, to adjust, to improve. Without the sting of falling short, it's easy to become complacent, to take success for granted. The struggle forces you to dig deeper, and that's where the real growth happens.

Life isn't about avoiding challenges—it's about embracing them. Think about learning a new skill, whether it's playing an instrument or training for a marathon. At first, it's awkward, uncomfortable. You hit roadblocks. You mess up. You wonder if you're making any progress. But then, after months or even years of struggle, there's that moment when it clicks, when everything comes together. And in that moment, all the previous frustration suddenly makes sense. You realize it was all part of the process, a necessary part of getting to where you are now.

Coach Wooden was right—the better days do come. It's inevitable, as long as you keep showing up, keep fighting, and keep pushing through. The storms pass, and eventually, the sun breaks through. But what I didn't realize then was that when those better days arrived, I would be grateful for the worse ones. Without those struggles, without those losses, our victory wouldn't have meant nearly as much.

In life, it's easy to focus on the end result, to think success is only about the final outcome. But the real magic lies in the journey—the times when you had to push yourself, when you questioned whether you were going to make it.

As you face your own challenges, remember this: The struggles you're enduring now are shaping you, preparing you for something greater. They're not obstacles to be avoided, but opportunities for growth. When you face setbacks in your career, your relationships, or your personal goals, remind yourself that these are the moments when you're being forged. They're the foundation of future success, even if it's not immediately clear.

Embrace them. Learn from them. Because one day, you'll look back and realize that these struggles were the most beautiful part of your journey.

They are what shaped you.

They are what made you.

To Study
Books

I don't know if you people like to read. I hated school
because I didn't want to read. All I do is read now,
but I read to learn.

—JERRY WEST

"Why did the slave masters hide their money in books, George?" Dear asked me as we stood together in her kitchen one day.

"I don't know, Grandma," I said.

"Because they knew the slaves wouldn't open them," she replied.

It's funny to me—over the years as I have told that story from my grandmother, some young people have tried to tell me that the story is racist. Or that it perpetuates a stereotype about "enslaved peoples." While I appreciate this newfound sensitivity, it misses the point. It also misses the fact that the story is very much true, however terrible that truth sounds.

My grandmother knew, in her own way, the dark relationship between slavery and literacy. In the antebellum South, teaching slaves to read was not only discouraged, it was illegal. States like Georgia, Alabama, and Virginia had laws imposing fines and even whippings on anyone caught teaching slaves to read or write. Books that were critical of slavery or humanized enslaved people were banned—for whites and Blacks—and anyone caught holding something like *Uncle Tom's Cabin* in Mississippi in the 1850s was taking a real risk of being lynched.

The ability to read was recognized as a form of power. If enslaved individuals learned to read and access information, it might inspire thoughts of freedom and rebellion. It might facilitate communication and the forging of plans to escape or resist slavery.

In the infamous words of Virginia's authoritarian governor William Berkeley, a slave owner who warned others like him to never educate enslaved people, "Learning has brought disobedience and heresy into the world . . . and libels against the best government."

Best government for who?

Berkeley wrote that in 1671, and through the 1800s, still, the vast majority of the nearly four million enslaved African Americans were illiterate. Then, brave and determined slaves like Frederick Douglass began to defy these unjust prohibitions, secretly teaching themselves and others to read, often using the Bible. "Knowledge is the pathway from slavery to freedom," as Douglass said. In his autobiography, *My Bondage and My Freedom*, he'd add, "I wished to learn how to write, as I might occasion to write my own pass."

There's a reason why enslaved people weren't allowed to read. There's a reason why cruel governments have always burned and banned books. Knowing things gives you power. This has been said so often it's now a platitude, but it contains within it another, even more important idea: Not knowing things makes you weak. It makes you dependent on others and less able to fight back when you're treated badly.

From this early lesson, I came to see reading as a moral duty. To not read, to remain in ignorance, was not only to be weak, it was to ignore the people who had fought so hard, who had struggled at such great cost to read and to provide for future generations the right and the ability to do so. It was to spit in the face of people like Frederick Douglass, Booker T. Washington, and Martin Luther King Jr.

My love affair with books truly began during my time at Villanova. Coming from a background where access to books had been limited, I found myself suddenly surrounded by a wealth of knowledge in the university library. It was like discovering a hidden treasure trove, and I was determined to make the most of it.

There was no such thing as the internet then—no Amazon, no Kindle, no audiobooks. Books were more beautiful—usually clothbound but often leatherbound—but as a result, they were not cheap and not always accessible. A library seemed to me to be a magical place. Unlimited books . . . for free? Again, remember: the fiction of segregation was "separate but equal." That's not how it was. Blacks were not welcomed at most libraries, and the ones we had access to were not the same. Richard Wright, who I wouldn't read until later, tells an incredible story in his memoir of forging a note as a young man that asked for books on behalf of a white coworker in order to read the writings of H. L. Mencken. He even referred to himself by the N-word to make the note seem more authentic!

At first, I stuck mainly to my textbooks, focusing on what I needed to know for my classes. But gradually, I began to explore other sections of the library. I'd wander the aisles, pulling out books that caught my eye, on subjects I'd never even heard of before. History, philosophy, science, literature—each book opened up a new world to me.

I remember stumbling upon *Up from Slavery* by Booker T. Washington and being transfixed. Here was the story of an African American born into hardship who rose through education and hard work. It resonated with my own experiences, yet it challenged me to think in new ways. I devoured biographies of great leaders, thinkers, and athletes, always looking for lessons I could apply to my own life. By the time I graduated, reading had become more than just a way to pass classes—it was a passion, a means of self-improvement, and a window to the wider world.

Looking back on that time, I can say without hesitation: Books liberated me. They became my GPS, guiding me through unfamiliar territories of knowledge and experience. They became my mentors, offering wisdom and insights from some of the greatest minds in history. They became my best friends, always there when I needed them, never judging, always ready to share their stories and ideas. Books took me places I had never been and taught me lessons I never would have learned on my own.

This liberation through literature was more than just metaphorical. Each book I read expanded my world, challenged my assumptions, and gave me new tools to navigate life's challenges. They provided me with a vocabulary to articulate my experiences and aspirations. They showed me possibilities I had never imagined for myself.

When I read about historical figures who had overcome tremendous odds, it gave me hope and courage to face my own obstacles. When I delved into books on strategy and leadership, I gained insights that would later prove invaluable in my coaching career. Even works of fiction broadened my empathy and understanding of the human condition in ways that would enrich my relationships and my approach to mentoring others.

Moreover, books became a great equalizer. In their pages, I could engage with ideas from the world's greatest thinkers on an equal footing. It didn't matter where I came from or what I looked like; what mattered was my willingness to grapple with the ideas, to think critically, to learn and grow.

This transformative relationship with books didn't end when I left college. If anything, it deepened as I entered the professional world. When I was a young man fresh out of Villanova, working my first job as a marketing analyst at Sunoco, I found myself surrounded for the first time by college-educated professionals. While my newfound love of reading had prepared me somewhat, I still felt the need to expand my knowledge further. Eager to engage in intelligent conversation and understand the world around me, I realized I needed to go beyond the books I had discovered in college. It was time to become an even more serious, systematic reader.

I made a commitment to myself: each day would include time for reading. Books became an essential part of my daily routine. I wasn't content to just read books—I studied them. When you read a book, you do it mainly for entertainment or general interest. But when you study a book, you engage with the material on a deeper level. You read with greater focus and intention, taking notes, asking questions, connecting ideas. You're not a passive consumer, but an active learner on a quest for knowledge and wisdom to apply to your life. My routine is to keep about five books going at a time on different topics: business, self-improvement, history, biographies, sports, anything that seems interesting. If I start a book and don't connect with it, I drop it, saying to myself, "This book doesn't want me right now. Maybe it will later." When a book does grab me, I'll devour it in a few sittings with a pen in hand. Over the years, I've developed my own system for studying books.

I circle anything that I want to research later—unfamiliar words, new concepts, people I want to learn more about. Then, after each reading session, I look up everything I've circled. In the margins, I draw horizontal lines next to paragraphs that are particularly important, passages I know I'll want to revisit two or three more times.

I also use different colored highlighters—I learned early on that using just one color does nothing for my brain. So I use pink, green, orange, and yellow, with each color representing something specific I'm tracking in the book. Orange might mark quotes I want to remember, pink might flag concepts I want to explore further outside the book. It might seem complex, but the color-coding helps me see connections and retain information better.

I use every blank page in a book too. Those empty pages in the back? I fill them with summaries, notes, and my own reflections on what I've read. After finishing the book, I transfer the most important insights into what I call my "learning journals," a practice I started in 1972. After many decades, I've accumulated dozens of these journals. I read not just to gather facts and information, but to broaden my perspective, to find solutions to problems, to shed light on the human condition. So I return to the learning journals often. I've used the valuable knowledge from the books I've studied over the past fifty years to make my living as a coach, as a businessman, and as a leader.

This system works for me, but every reader develops their own way of reading. Books teach you how to think, not what to think.

Our education system is geared toward the latter, but I've realized that books are a path to liberation. Every time I pick up a book, I feel a unique freedom—the joy of discovery, where I can make up my own rules about even how to read them.

My approach to reading has evolved into what some might call an obsession. I never go anywhere without a book and a notebook. Whether I'm in the waiting room at the doctor's office or standing in a checkout queue, I'm reading. I've even developed a new system: if I'm in a bookstore and the line is long, I'll start reading and underlining right there in line. It's all part of my mission to make every moment an opportunity for learning.

Over the years, I've developed a unique approach to reading that maximizes my learning and engagement with the material. I don't always start at the beginning and read straight through to the end. Instead, I divide the book into messages. I'll go to the table of contents, find what I believe is an interesting chapter, and start there. This approach allows me to focus on the most powerful and influential parts of the book, rather than getting bogged down in less impactful sections.

My book selection process is equally methodical. I have a routine when I enter my local Barnes & Noble bookstore, which I do several times a week, every week. First, I check the books on sale. Then I move to the new releases in nonfiction. I'll pick up a book, read about the author, check the promotional blurbs, and then dive into a chapter to get a sense of the writer's style. I'm looking for books that will change the way I think, act, or behave. Those are the ones that ultimately have the most impact on me. That said, the books I choose never conform to one genre. If I'm reading four books at once, one might be a biography of Ben Franklin, one might be a leadership book written by a CEO I respect, one might be a scientific study of the brain, and one might be a sports memoir. It's vitally important to read as widely as possible and to explore topics outside your comfort zone. This is how reading leads to growth.

I've found that even intimidatingly large books can be conquered with the right approach. I see them as a personal challenge, an opportunity rather than an obstacle. For instance, a seven-hundred-page tome might seem daunting, but if you approach it strategically—say, reading it during a long flight—suddenly it becomes manageable. For some books, you just have to find the right environment in which to read them.

This voracious appetite for reading has earned me the nickname the "Human Google" among some of my friends and colleagues. But more important, it's given me a vast reservoir of knowledge to draw from in my work as a coach, mentor, and educator. I've found that the wisdom gleaned from books can be applied to countless real-world situations, from motivating a team to navigating complex business challenges.

As you journey through this book, you'll notice that my love for reading has deeply influenced my approach to storytelling and teaching. Throughout these pages, you'll encounter a tapestry of wisdom woven from diverse threads—personal anecdotes, historical events, literary references, and even mythological tales. This isn't just a stylistic choice; it reflects the way I've come to understand and interpret the world through my lifelong dedication to reading. I've pulled much of this wisdom from my home library, where I've amassed thousands of books.

You might find yourself transported to ancient Greece one moment, contemplating the ethical dilemmas faced by Socrates, and in the next, you'll be on the sidelines of a crucial basketball game, learning about leadership and teamwork. You'll meet characters from classic literature who embody timeless virtues, and you'll hear echoes of great speeches that have shaped our world. These varied examples serve a purpose beyond mere illustration—they demonstrate how the lessons of history, the insights of great thinkers, and the archetypes of myth can illuminate our own experiences and challenges.

This approach stems from my belief that true wisdom isn't confined to a single discipline or era. By drawing connections between seemingly disparate ideas—say, a principle of physics and a coaching strategy, or an ancient philosophical concept and a modern business practice—we can uncover deeper truths about human nature and the world around us.

As you encounter these diverse references, I encourage you to approach them with the same curiosity and openness that I've cultivated in my reading habit. Let them spark your imagination, challenge your assumptions, and inspire you to delve deeper into subjects that pique your interest. In doing so, you'll be embarking on your own journey of lifelong learning, one that can enrich your understanding and broaden your perspective in ways you might never have anticipated.

Remember, the examples and stories you'll find in this book are not just illustrations—they're invitations. Invitations to explore new ideas, to question your existing beliefs, and to see the world through different lenses. They're proof of the transformative power of reading, and of the endless possibilities that open up when we approach life with an inquiring mind and a well-stocked library.

I encourage everyone I meet, especially young people, to develop their own reading habit. It doesn't matter where you start— what matters is that you start. Pick up a book that interests you, dive in, and see where it takes you. You might just find, as I have, that books can be the key to unlocking your potential and expanding your understanding of the world.

Remember, in a world where information is readily available at our fingertips, the ability to deeply engage with ideas, to synthesize information, and to apply knowledge creatively is more valuable than ever. And there's no better way to develop these skills than through the dedicated study of books.

So, it is worth pointing out: just like that old story my grandmother used to tell me, money really is hidden in the pages of books. The difference is that the only person keeping you from that money is you. If you want to get better at just about anything, if you want to extricate yourself from a cycle of mediocrity, if you want solutions to your problems—study books. Study books because it will make you powerful. Study books because if you don't, you will become weak—easy to manipulate, less than what you are capable of being.

It's in your self-interest to study books (there's money in it).

It's your moral duty to study books.

And it's what you were made for. As I said: with two ears and one mouth, we were made to listen more than we talk. And since we also have two eyes, we were made to read and observe more than we talk as well.

Our eyes allow us to read, but our mouth can only regurgitate a fraction of what we take in.

We were made to read more than we speak.

We were made to fill our minds with the wisdom of books.

We were made to study books.

To Dispense Love

Keep love in your heart. A life without it is like a sunless garden when the flowers are dead. The consciousness of loving and being loved brings a warmth and richness to life that nothing else can bring.

—OSCAR WILDE

It was the late 1950s, and I was a senior at Villanova. We were headed to Morgantown to face off against West Virginia University and their hometown hero, Jerry West. Little did I know, this trip would become a defining moment in my life, a testament to the power of love in the face of hatred and fear.

As our train rolled into Morgantown, I couldn't shake the sense of unease that had been building in my gut. This was the South, after all, a place where the color of my skin made me a target, a threat, an outsider. But I tried to focus on the game ahead, on the opportunity to compete against one of the best players in the country.

When we arrived at the field house in Morgantown, the tension was palpable. As the only two Black players on the Villanova squad, Hubie White and I drew stares and murmurs from the all-white crowd. I could feel their eyes boring into me, could hear the whispers of "nigger" and worse echoing off the walls.

But when the game began, all that faded away. It was just me, the ball, and the man I was assigned to guard, Jerry West himself. He was a blur of motion, a scoring machine that seemed unstoppable. But I was determined to prove myself, to show that I belonged on the same court as this future legend.

Late in the game, with Villanova trailing, I found myself chasing West on a fast break. He went up for a layup, and I leaped with everything I had, sending both of us crashing into the stands. As we lay there tangled together, the field house fell silent. I could feel the eyes of the crowd on us, could sense the anger and hostility crackling in the air. In that moment, I feared for my life.

But then, something extraordinary happened. Jerry West, the golden boy of West Virginia, the pride of Morgantown, reached out his hand to me. And as he pulled me to my feet, the crowd began to applaud. In that simple gesture, he had defused the tension, had shown that on the court, we were equals, competitors, worthy of respect.

I fouled out of the game a few minutes later, my dreams of a victory over West shattered. But as I made my way to the bench, something even more remarkable occurred. West chased me down, caught me by the arm, and shook my hand. "Good game," he said, looking me square in the eye. "It was a pleasure playing against you."

I was stunned. Here was this white man, this hero to the people who had just been calling me every slur in the book, treating me with dignity and respect. Showing me, in front of everyone, that he saw me as a human being, as someone worthy of compassion and kindness.

That moment marked the beginning of a friendship that would endure for over half a century. Though we only spoke a handful of times over the years, the bond we forged on that court in Morgantown never faded. Jerry would go on to become an NBA legend, the silhouette behind the league's iconic logo. But to me, he was always the man who had the courage to reach out, to bridge the divide of race and prejudice with a simple act of decency.

Years later, in a conversation captured for a documentary, Jerry reflected on that game and what it meant to him. "You know, it's really interesting to hear you talk about that one day in particular in our lives," he said to me. "People today wouldn't even believe it, how the progression of time, the advent of our modern-day athletes, the enormous appeal that they have."

He paused for a moment, then continued. "I want you to know, you were the first Black person I ever played against. That seems hard to believe. And thinking back about that day in the locker room, you had a good team. And obviously I had no idea you had Hubie White with you, another Black man who was a terrific player himself."

Jerry went on to describe the tension of that day, the undercurrent of racism that permeated the crowd. "West Virginia, it's a border state, but it's very much a Southern state," he explained. "And at that point in time, I'll never forget, when you went up for that shot and ended up over there by the stands, that floor was hard as a rock. It wasn't fun to play on."

But then he said something that struck me to my core. "That was really a day that I think I'll never forget," he said. "And I was so grateful that again, nothing happened, but more that it showed that competition mattered. It doesn't matter who you are, it doesn't matter what race you are. It's about people who want to compete and win. There was no ulterior motive in it to make anyone look bad."

Hearing Jerry describe that game, the significance of that moment, through his eyes, was a revelation. It affirmed what I had always believed about him, about the purity of his love for the game and the depth of his character.

He could have easily seen me as a threat, as an opponent to be vanquished at all costs. But instead, he saw me as an equal, a competitor worthy of respect and dignity. Even in the midst of a dominant performance—"I had a big scoring day that day," he recalled with a chuckle—his focus was on the larger meaning of our interaction, the way it transcended the boundaries of sport and society.

That, to me, is the true measure of Jerry West's greatness. Not just his skill on the court, but his humanity off it. His willingness to see beyond the color of a person's skin, to connect with them on a level of shared passion and mutual respect.

Jerry passed away during the writing of this book. When I heard of his passing, it hit me like a ton of bricks. I couldn't control my emotions, couldn't stem the flood of memories and gratitude that poured out of me. I shut off my phone and retreated into myself, trying to make sense of what his loss meant to me, to the world.

In the days that followed, as I reflected on Jerry's life and our friendship, I realized that he had taught me one of the most valuable lessons of my life: that love is the most powerful force we possess. That in the face of hatred, of ignorance, of fear, love is the only answer. It is the bridge that connects us, the light that guides us through the darkness.

Jerry West showed me the power of loving those who others

deem unlovable. Of extending compassion and respect to those who have been denied it. Of using our privilege and platform to lift up the marginalized and oppressed.

In my own life, I've tried to carry that lesson with me, to be a dispenser of love in a world that so desperately needs it. Whether it's telling my friends and family that I love them, supporting young athletes who are striving to make their dreams a reality, or speaking out against injustice and bigotry, I've tried to live my life in a way that honors Jerry's example.

Because at the end of the day, that's what we're all called to do. To love one another, without reservation or hesitation. To see the humanity in every person we encounter, no matter how different they may seem. To use whatever power and influence we have to make this world a little bit brighter, a little bit more just, a little bit kinder.

It's a lesson that I've carried with me throughout my life, and one that I believe we could all stand to learn from today. In a world that is all too often divided by race, by class, by ideology, we need more people like Jerry West. People who are willing to reach across those divides, to see the humanity in one another, to compete with grace and compassion.

That's the legacy that Jerry leaves behind, and it's one I will always cherish. Not just as a basketball player, but as a man, as a friend, as a shining example of what it means to dispense love in the face of hate, unity in the face of division, light in the face of darkness.

It's not always easy. There are times when the darkness seems overwhelming, when hate and division threaten to swallow us whole. But in those moments, I think back to that day in Morgantown, to the hand that Jerry extended to me, and I find the strength to keep going, to keep loving, to keep dispensing light.

That's the legacy that Jerry West left behind. Not just the championships and the accolades, but the way he treated people, the way he used his gifts to make the world a better place. And it's a legacy that we can all aspire to, no matter who we are or where we come from.

Be a dispenser of love. In your homes, in your communities, in your places of work and worship. Seek out the forgotten and the marginalized, the hurting and the hopeless, and show them that they matter, that they are seen and valued and loved.

Because in the end, that's what we're all here for. To love and be loved, to lift each other up, to leave this world a little bit better than we found it.

It won't be easy. There will be moments of fear and doubt, of anger and despair. But if we can hold fast to love, if we can remember the example of those like Jerry West who came before us, then I believe there is nothing we cannot achieve, no barrier we cannot break down, no wound we cannot heal.

So go forth and love. Dispense it freely, without fear or reservation. It is the most powerful tool we have, the most precious gift we can give.

And in doing so, we honor the memory of those who taught us how to love, and we build a world where love truly conquers all.

To Serve Others

Goodness is the only investment that
never fails.

—HENRY DAVID THOREAU

Around the age of eighty, I made a pivotal, conscious decision that would transform the rest of my life. I said to myself, "I'm going to spend the rest of my life being a servant
to other people. It's not about me anymore. It's about everyone else."

This wasn't a completely new concept for me. Throughout my
career as a coach and mentor, I had always tried to help others. I had
often told my players, "If all I teach you is how to be a great basketball player, you should have gone somewhere else. I want this to be a
unique experience. I want you to be better because you'll be around
me, and I want to be a better person because I'll be around you."

But I realized that subconsciously, the pursuit of success, money,
and influence had been driving many of my decisions. These weren't
explicit goals, but they were there, shaping my choices in ways I
hadn't fully appreciated.

With this new awareness, I restructured my life around being a servant leader, helping as many people as possible live better lives. This shift led me to develop what I now call my magic question: "What can I do for you?"

It's a simple question, but it's become a cornerstone of my daily interactions. I must ask this magic question twenty times a day— to friends, to strangers, to anyone I interact with. Some people take me up on the offer immediately, but most don't. The key is to ask sincerely and be prepared to follow through when someone does take you up on it.

I remember one day, I got a call from an old friend. "Coach," he said, "you know how you always said if there's anything you can do for me? Well, I finally found something." It was a moment of truth—I had written a check, and now it was time to cash it. Was there a part of me that was a little scared about what the request was going to be? Sure. Just like you, my wife and I have been pitched plenty of bad investment ideas, and people have asked us to do some crazy stuff, but I'm not really talking about that.

Not everything we've been asked to do has been easy or fun, but that's the beauty of service—it's not about convenience, it's about commitment.

Just as I have dedicated my life to serving others in my professional career, I've always tried to apply the same principles at home. Being a husband and a father isn't just about providing; it's about serving. My family is my most important team, and I strive to lead by example, offering support, love, and guidance whenever it's needed. The same magic question I ask in my professional life, "What can I do for you?" is something I often reflect on in my family life. Whether it's being there for my children when they need advice or supporting my wife through her own endeavors, I've learned that the most meaningful service starts at home.

It was early in my coaching career when I first met Freddie Lewis, the head coach at Syracuse University during the 1960s. I was in the habit of seeking out insights from successful coaches and leaders, people who had walked the path I was just beginning to navigate. So when I found myself at a high school game with Freddie one evening, I asked him if he had any words of wisdom.

"Don't ever forget that I told you this," he said without hesitation. "Plant a lot of flowers on the way up, because you're going to have to pick them on the way down."

I've shared Freddie's advice with countless other coaches I've mentored over the years. I imagine them shaking their heads as they read this because they hear me say it so often: always be planting flowers because you're eventually going to have to pick some. Be of service, make positive contributions to your relationships, spread kindness, support others, create a foundation of goodwill. Life has its ups and downs, and the seeds we sow during our high points will be the support we lean on during the low points.

Even in the business world, during my time as an executive at Nike, I found that this service mindset was the key to effective leadership. It wasn't about wielding power or authority, but about empowering others to do their best work. It was about taking the time to really see and hear the people around you—to ask questions, to learn their stories, to understand their hopes and dreams.

Phil Knight was a master at this. He had an uncanny ability to connect with people from all walks of life, to make them feel valued and inspired. I remember one trip we took to China back in 1975, long before it was a regular stop on the global business circuit. Phil was endlessly curious, always eager to learn and to build bridges across cultural divides. That experience opened my eyes to a whole new world of possibility, and it reinforced the idea that great leaders are, at their core, great teammates.

Service to others extends far beyond the court or the office; it's about investing in the people around you, helping them grow and succeed. I remember when one of my players was struggling academically, and there was a real concern that he might not be eligible to play. Instead of just letting him handle it on his own, I sat down with him and his professors to work out a plan. We created a schedule that balanced his academic workload with his training, and I made it a point to check in with him regularly, not just on his performance on the court, but on how he was managing his studies. It wasn't about winning games; it was about ensuring that he succeeded as a student and as a person. That's what true service is about—seeing the whole person and being willing to invest in their growth, no matter the cost.

Of course, being of service isn't always about grand gestures or big-picture vision. Often, it's about the small, everyday acts of kindness and connection that can make all the difference in someone's life.

I make it a point to compliment people whenever I can, to let them know that they're seen and appreciated. Just the other day, I noticed that a waitress at one of my regular restaurants had done her hair differently. "I really like the way you have your hair," I told her, and her face lit up with surprise and delight. "Wow, that's so nice of you to say," she replied.

It's such a simple thing, but in a world where so many people go through their days feeling invisible or unvalued, a kind word can be a powerful force. It's about taking a moment to really see the person in front of you, to acknowledge their humanity and their worth.

That's why I've made it a habit to learn the names of the people who serve me in restaurants, to ask about their families and their lives. It's why I take the time to chat with the drivers who shuttle me to meetings and events, to hear their stories and perspectives. And it's why, on Mother's Day a few years back, I stopped to buy flowers for all the moms working at my favorite breakfast spot.

"You didn't have to do that," one of the waitresses told me, her eyes welling up with tears. "That means so much to us."

But again, being of service isn't about obligation or expectation.

It's about recognizing that we are all interconnected and that supporting each other is a fundamental part of our nature.

This may sound abstract and philosophical, but it's actually a practical reality that can transform our lives when we fully embrace and act upon it. I discovered this truth firsthand around the age of eighty.

One of the interesting and unexpected by-products of committing the rest of my life to being a servant to others was a renewed enthusiasm for learning and self-education. As I engaged with people from all walks of life, listening to their stories, challenges, and aspirations, I quickly realized how much I still had to learn. Each interaction became an opportunity for growth, exposing me to new perspectives, ideas, and ways of thinking.

To truly be of service, I needed to continually expand my knowledge and understanding. This realization ignited a thirst for learning that surpassed anything I had experienced before. I found myself voraciously reading, asking questions, and seeking out new experiences, all in service of being better equipped to help others.

By dedicating myself to others' growth and well-being, I discovered a path to continue reaching my own outer limits as a human being. I uncovered new dimensions of myself and new ways to grow. This experience reinforced my belief in our fundamental interconnectedness. As I served others, I grew. As I helped others improve their lives, my own life was enriched. It was a powerful reminder that when we support each other, we all rise together.

This shift in both how I think and how I spend my time and energy transformed my later years into some of the most fulfilling and enlightening of my life.

And it solidified my belief that we were put on this earth not just to serve ourselves, but to serve others.

To be a force for good in the lives of those around us.

To focus less on what we can achieve for ourselves and more on how we can show up for others.

To offer a helping hand or a listening ear.

To be a good teammate.

To plant flowers.

To serve others.

To Keep
Hope Alive

Hope is the thing with feathers
That perches in the soul,
And sings the tune without the words,
And never stops at all,

—EMILY DICKINSON

On August 26, 1963, I was having dinner at my best friend Warren Wilson's home in Claymont, Delaware, a suburb of Wilmington. In the background, the television was on with news commentary about the upcoming March on Washington for Jobs and Freedom. Warren's dad, a prominent dentist in Wilmington, asked, "Are you boys going to go to the March on Washington?"

No, we said, offering some excuse about not having money or a way to get there. It was true I didn't have much money, but honestly, I was twenty-six, and just caught up in my own life. Like I said, I'd grown up in a predominantly Black city and been consumed by my own family's issues. Then, during my formative years, I attended a Catholic boarding school near Scranton, Pennsylvania, in a more isolated, insulated environment. It wasn't the kind of place where I encountered the same racial dynamics or diversity that I might have in a bigger city. In a way, I was cut off from the realities others were dealing with in the wider world.

It seems crazy to say this now, but I think in my very ordinary youthful self-absorption, I didn't exactly know what this march had to do with me. I figured other people were on top of the issue and if it pertained to me, someone would say something.

Thankfully, that person was Dr. Wilson.

"Well, this is going to be a historic event," he explained. "It could be the largest gathering of Black people in the history of America in one place." He offered to lend us one of the two family cars, along with some money for the trip.

The next day, Warren and I took off for Washington, D.C. At that time, the main road into the city was Route 1, which led into New York Avenue. Along the way, we found a motel suitable to our budget (and that would in fact rent a room to two Black men) and dropped off our bags. Eager and excited, we decided to head down to the National Mall that evening to scope out the location and plan our route for the morning.

As we walked around the grounds of the Lincoln Memorial, a gentleman stopped us and asked if we were planning to attend tomorrow. "Absolutely," we said.

"Would you want to volunteer?" he asked.

"For what?"

"To be security guards."

He explained that they were now expecting over a hundred thousand people, double the original predictions, and needed extra help with crowd control. We said we'd be happy to assist, and he instructed, "Meet me down here tomorrow morning at eight fifteen."

The next morning, we woke up filled with excitement and

anticipation. When we arrived on-site, it was already buzzing with early arrivals, and the organizer was relieved to see us. He ushered us over to a tent, where we were briefed on our duties and given white cardboard hats to wear for identification, marking us as part of the security detail. Because of our size (both Warren and I were six feet, four inches), we were assigned to the podium where the speakers would be addressing the crowd.

My job was to provide security for the dignitaries, to ensure that no one could get to them. In retrospect, I find it interesting that we weren't really given specific instructions on how to handle potential threats. They didn't tell us to wrestle anyone down or use force. I'm not exactly sure if they expected us to follow the principles of nonviolence or if we were the exception to the rule . . . or if we were just for show. They did tell us over and over again that our primary job was to prevent harm to the people on the podium.

What many people don't know is the extent of the security measures in place that day. President Kennedy had two army brigades on full alert, in full gear, stationed at one of the army bases near Arlington, Virginia. They were ready to move at a moment's notice if things got out of hand.

Moreover, the crowd around us was peppered with undercover law enforcement. I'd estimate that about 80 percent of the people you'd see dressed in white caps or civilian clothes near the podium were either FBI or Secret Service agents. The government was taking no chances with an event of this magnitude and potential volatility.

Still, what would I have done had someone rushed the stage? I have no idea. I was practically trembling with excitement and adrenaline anyway. I'm not sure how much good I would have been. But I felt there on those steps that my job was important, and although I'd played basketball in front of some large crowds, I had never seen this many people in my life.

The atmosphere was electric, with a tangible sense that we were on the cusp of something momentous. As the morning progressed, the crowd swelled to unimaginable numbers. People poured in from all directions. Buses and trains emptied thousands of marchers. Others arrived on foot, some having walked for miles, but it didn't matter: with the spirit of unity and purpose in the air, everyone was smiling.

Surveying the scene from my post near the stage, I marveled that for all the diversity, the mass of people seemed like one single living organism. There were people of all ages and races, from every walk of life—students and laborers, clergy and activists, parents pushing strollers and elderly folks in wheelchairs. Gospel choirs belted out freedom songs. Anthems like "We Shall Overcome" echoed across the National Mall. Marchers carried signs with slogans like "Jobs and Freedom" and "We March for Integrated Schools Now!"

They were here to make *demands*, and yet everywhere, what one felt was the dignity, discipline, and hope of all these Americans.

The program featured a series of influential speakers, from march organizer A. Philip Randolph declaring it "the greatest demonstration for freedom in the history of our nation" to John Lewis of the Student Nonviolent Coordinating Committee delivering a fiery call to action. I would learn later that his original speech promised a Shermanesque March to the Sea in pursuit of racial justice, but he had been forced to tone it down.

The headliner, every student now knows, was Dr. Martin Luther King Jr., whose oratorical skills were reason enough to endure the sweltering August heat until the very end. He was introduced to a thunderous ovation. Press photographers jostled for position, their flashbulbs popping. Reporters from around the globe leaned in, pens poised over their notepads.

Dr. King approached the podium with a solemn, purposeful stride. He was impeccably dressed in a dark suit, crisp white shirt, and a black tie. As he arranged his notes on the lectern, which was adorned with a colorful array of microphones bearing the insignia of the major television and radio networks, he appeared to take a deep, centering breath.

I moved to a vantage point from which I could see the beads of sweat glistening on his brow. It was partially because of the afternoon sun, but more likely, it was the weight of the moment settling onto his shoulders. But when he gripped the sides of the podium and looked out at the sea of expectant faces, there was a transformation. As he began to speak, it was as if a higher power had taken hold of him and Martin Luther King Jr., the man, was now merely a conduit, a vessel chosen to deliver a message of historic significance. His voice, always powerful, took on an otherworldly resonance. His eyes, usually kind and gentle, blazed with the fire of prophecy. His entire being vibrated with urgency, the importance of this divine message.

I was mesmerized. The cadence, the rise and fall of his rich baritone voice, the poetry of his language, the timing of his pauses—I hung on every second of it. I realized I was in a total trance when it was interrupted by a female voice on the other side of the podium,

"Tell them about the dream, Martin," it said. "Tell them about the dream."

Tell them about the dream.

Even just thinking of that phrase now fills me with goose bumps. For a fleeting moment I had been so close to these Olympian gods, these beautiful, magical figures who changed the world. It almost seems like a dream itself. I looked over, and seated with other guests of honor, I saw the owner of that melodious voice. It was Mahalia Jackson, the legendary gospel singer.

Mahalia had been a close confidante and spiritual support to Dr. King throughout the Civil Rights Movement. Their friendship was so deep that when Dr. King was weary or disheartened, he would call Mahalia and ask her to sing to him over the phone. Her powerful voice, rich with the cadences of the church, never failed to lift his spirits and refill him with hope. "He would listen to her voice, and sometimes tears would come down his face," one of King's biographers, Clarence B. Jones, writes. "She was not just his favorite gospel singer, she was practically his muse."

King paused, looked over at his muse, down at his prepared remarks, then up at the crowd. He leaned forward and began to improvise:

"I have a dream . . . It is a dream deeply rooted in the American dream."

He had a dream of a future where this nation would rise up and live out the true meaning of its creed: that all men are created equal. He envisioned a day when the sons of former slaves and the sons of former slave owners could sit down together at the table of brother- and sisterhood. He dreamed of a time when the states rife with injustice and oppression would be transformed into an oasis of freedom and justice. He longed for a future where his four children would be judged by their character rather than the color of their skin. Where Black and white children would join hands as siblings. Where every valley would be exalted, every hill and mountain made low, and the vicious and crooked places made decent and straight.

He was riffing, but like a great jazz musician, he knew where he was going; he had explored similar territory a thousand times for a thousand audiences. He knew which notes to hit. He knew which themes counted. He knew his philosophy, his religion, and his politics, and there with the world watching, it came together as one. And yet, I believe he was also touched in this moment by some force beyond. Have a man and a moment merged more beautifully? More perfectly? And to think he was doing it live, on the razor's edge . . . it's staggering. Transcendent.

It and he belong to the ages.

"And when this happens," he said, "and when we allow freedom to ring, when we let it ring from every village and every hamlet, from every state and every city, we will be able to speed up that day when all of God's children, Black men and white men, Jews and Gentiles, Protestants and Catholics, will be able to join hands and sing in the words of the old Negro spiritual: Free at last! Free at last! Thank God Almighty, we are free at last!"

After that unforgettable closing refrain, the crowd exploded. Dr. King folded up his speech and made his way off the podium in my direction. Without really thinking about what I was doing, I stepped forward and asked, "Dr. King, could I have that copy of the speech?" And I think without really thinking about what he was doing, he handed it to me. Just as he handed it to me, Archbishop Patrick O'Boyle, who delivered the invocation, made a comment to Dr. King about how powerful and inspiring the speech had been, shifting his attention away from my extraordinary souvenir.

I'll never forget standing there on those marble steps watching Dr. King build a multiracial community of hope and possibility in real time. And I'll never forget the sense of excitement that swelled in me as I realized that one person can use their voice and conviction to stir the hearts and minds of hundreds of thousands.

I was there. I touched him. He touched me. *It happened.*

Part of the reason I had not been inclined to go to the march was that I simply assumed the world was the way it was. That there were some good white people (like those who had opened doors for me) and some bad ones and that things were always going to be this way. I wasn't hopeless or anything, but I was not a hopeful person. Dear had made sure that I was not naive. The loss of my parents had made me see the world a certain way—and let's just say, it wasn't the most cheerful view.

What Dr. King gave me, then, was hope. He had outlined a stirring vision for a world very different from the one we then knew. He had told us his dream, which was really an inconceivable one at that time, but he believed it. His words were a call to responsibility: to hope and dream of a better future, and to believe that future was truly possible, if we had the courage to work for it.

To give someone hope? What an incredible gift.

In the years that followed, I tried to pay forward that gift.

At Washington State, I coached a kid named James Donaldson. A 7′2″ center out of Sacramento, James had received no other scholarship offers when I convinced him to come play for me.

I'd heard about James through a junior college coach who simply said, "Hey, I heard there's a seven-footer over at Burbank High. I never saw him play, but you might want to check on him." When I did, the high school coach told me, "He's never played basketball before. He's a work in progress."

That didn't deter me. Everyone's a work in progress. When I met James, I saw something beyond his physical stature. There was a quiet determination in his eyes, a humility in his demeanor, and an eagerness to learn that got me excited.

He wasn't sure he was a college-level basketball player, but I was proud of my ability to give him the hope that he could be. I offered James a scholarship and he took it. The high school coach couldn't believe it. Later, he asked me, "Coach, can you tell me what you see in James?"

James had qualities that were far more valuable than raw talent, I said. I'd seen gifted athletes squander their potential because they lacked the character to match their abilities. But James was different. He listened intently, asked thoughtful questions, and showed a genuine desire to put in the work to improve. When I mentioned to James that while he had the potential to be great, he would need to put in an enormous amount of work to catch up to players who had been playing organized basketball for years, his response told me everything I needed to know. His eyes lit up with anticipation. He didn't make excuses for his lack of experience or try to coast on his height alone. Instead, he expressed a sincere commitment to putting in the work. He needed help to succeed, and I wanted to be the person to do that. I knew that if I put the time in, if I invested in James not just as a player but as a person, the returns would be extraordinary.

James accepted the scholarship offer, and I brought him to Pullman for the summer, got him a job, and worked with him at the gym every day. We initially agreed that he would redshirt his freshman year, but by the time we got ready to start the season, James had made amazing progress. As the season approached, I realized he could actually contribute in games, so we decided to take the redshirt off.

He transformed from a raw recruit into a formidable player.

During his time at Washington State, James became the best shot blocker in school history, setting a single-game record with ten blocks against Seattle University in 1977. He broke his own records for blocks and blocks per game in both his junior and senior years. On the other end of the court, he averaged a double-double for points and rebounds over his junior and senior seasons, pulling down 305 rebounds as a junior—a mark that ranked second on the WSU single-season list when he left Pullman.

But his success wasn't limited to the basketball court. As a student-athlete, James exemplified the term in every sense. He approached his academics with the same determination he showed in practice. I never once had to worry about his grades or class attendance. If you told James to do something—whether it was extra drills after practice or a paper for his business class—you could walk away knowing it was going to get done, and done well.

James graduated in four years with a degree in business administration, a proud moment for him as the first in his family to earn a college degree. His growth, as both a player and a person, was remarkable to witness.

His hard work and development at Washington State caught the eye of NBA scouts, and he was drafted by the Seattle Super-Sonics in the fourth round of the 1979 NBA draft. What followed was an impressive fourteen-year NBA career that saw him play for several teams, including the Los Angeles Clippers, Dallas Mavericks, New York Knicks, and Utah Jazz. He led the NBA in field goal percentage at 63.7 percent in 1985 and was selected as an All-Star in 1988. By the end of his professional career, James had scored 8,203 points and pulled down 7,492 rebounds, solidifying his place in basketball history.

James's legacy in college basketball was further cemented when he was inducted into the Pac-10 Men's Basketball Hall of Honor in 2006.

But I'm not telling you this story to show that I helped turn a guy into a pro athlete. That's a unique experience that I've had many times in my life. It's not easy to do but enough people have done it that it's not that special. James and I came into each other's lives for something much more important that.

One day, decades after I coached him, James called me. I could tell immediately that something was terribly wrong. I found out later that he had come home from a trip to discover his wife had left him, taking their young child and most of the valuables from the house. He didn't tell me any of this on the phone; in fact, if I remember right, he went out of his way to tell me that things were going well and everything was good with him.

I could tell this was all a lie, though. I could hear the despair in his voice. Calling me was his way of saying goodbye because he was going to kill himself.

He was in over his head financially. He was racked with guilt and shame and then suddenly his entire support system had crumbled. I didn't know any of this exactly, I just knew I was talking to someone who was in trouble and I knew my job was to keep him talking, to bring him a little bit back from whatever edge he was on. I kept him on the phone and then drove to see him.

Now, if this were a movie, you might expect a dramatic scene where I, as the wise old coach, deliver some life-changing, inspiring speech that instantly pulls James back from the brink. But real life isn't like that. Hope, I've learned, often comes in much quieter, more mundane forms.

What actually happened was far simpler, yet in many ways,

more profound. It was a day-to-day process. I'd say to myself, "Just help him get through the day." "Just take it one day at a time."

This is also what James had been like as a player. His coach had told me he was a work in progress, and I had just tried to see him through each practice. In life and on the court, slowly, steadily, those days, that effort will add up. From that day forward, I made a commitment to call James every day, sometimes twice a day. If he needed money or help with something, I gave it. I tried to use my voice and my conviction to alter his heart and his mind, to get him to hope and dream of a better future and to believe that it was truly possible. But mostly, I was just there, a constant presence reminding him that he wasn't alone.

You see, hope isn't always delivered in grand gestures or rousing speeches. It's not always an "I Have a Dream" moment. Sometimes, hope is as simple as giving someone a reason to get through until morning. It's quiet persistence. It's small, consistent acts. It's showing up, day after day, and saying, "I'm here for you."

This is the kind of hope that doesn't make headlines or inspire crowds, but it's the kind that saves lives, that rebuilds them one day at a time. It's the hope that says, "You matter, your life has value, and I'm not giving up on you."

That was the commitment I made to James all those years ago when I first recruited him. Investing in someone—truly investing in their growth and well-being—isn't confined to a specific time frame or context. It's a lifelong commitment. The "work in progress" I had seen in that young, inexperienced basketball player was still ongoing, and I was still willing to put in the time.

James not only overcame his struggles but went on to new challenges and achievements. He became an author, opening up about his battles with depression, his suicidal thoughts, and his journey that had brought him from the depths of despair to a place of hope and purpose in a book titled *Celebrating Your Gift of Life*. He became a vocal advocate for mental health awareness and continues to do a lot of public speaking, sharing his story and helping others who might be struggling. He became a leader in his community, even running for mayor of Seattle (he lost in a close election).

In many ways, James had come full circle. The young man who once needed hope and support had become a beacon of hope for others, extending the very kind of lifeline that had been offered to him in his darkest hours. It's a remarkable journey—from raw basketball recruit to NBA player, from someone who contemplated ending it all to a politician, and then to a voice of hope for others. And it's a powerful reminder of the resilience of the human spirit and the importance of having someone who believes in you.

In every era of history and in all walks of life, there are challenges that seem insurmountable, problems that seem unsolvable, times when the hardship seems permanent, and moments when the darkness seems to be never-ending.

In every era of history and in all walks of life, we need people like Dr. King—people who use their voice and their conviction to help others believe that a better future is possible, that the problems we face are solvable, that there is light at the end of the long, dark tunnel.

We need people like Mahalia Jackson—people who others know they can call when they're having a rough day. People who can remind you of the dream, who can call you down from the depths and up to the mountaintop.

We need friends and coaches and mentors and confidants who lift us up with their words, their songs, their prayers, and their unwavering presence when we feel like we can't go on, when the weight of the world feels too heavy to bear.

We need people who keep hope alive.

In my years of coaching and mentoring, I've come to realize that small, everyday actions can make a profound difference in someone's life.

Each day is composed of 86,400 seconds—that's 86,400 opportunities to make ourselves better than we were yesterday, to bring hope to someone else. These opportunities can be as simple as offering a genuine "thank you," sharing a warm smile, or giving an encouraging pat on the back.

It's sobering to think that there are people who go an entire day without hearing a single positive word. But that also means each of us has the power, every single day, to be that positive voice for someone. We have 86,400 chances daily to spark hope in another person's life.

Keeping hope alive isn't just about being there in someone's darkest hour, like I was for James. It's also about those small, consistent acts of kindness and encouragement that can light up someone's day. Whether it's Dr. King inspiring a nation, Mahalia Jackson lifting spirits with her voice, or simply you offering a kind word to a stranger—we all have the capacity to be hope givers.

In the end, that's what we're made for—to lift each other up, to remind each other of our inherent worth and potential, to keep hope alive in big ways and small.

Every second of every day, we have the opportunity to fulfill this purpose. Let's make the most of it.

To Be
a Friend

We need more light about each other.
Light creates understanding, understanding creates love,
love creates patience, and patience creates unity.

—MALCOLM X

Often people ask, "How do you account for all the great things that have happened to you in your life?"

And the one word I use to capture it all is *relationships*.

My whole life has been built on relationships. The people I've met, the friendships I've cultivated, the players I've coached, the athletic directors I've worked for: these are the bricks my life is built on.

When I was interviewing for the head coaching job at Washington State, at one point, I asked the athletic director, "Why do you want me? How did you even find out about me?"

"I felt that we need someone who can get players," he said, "not necessarily someone who can out-coach other coaches. And every time I ask somebody, 'Who's the best recruiter you know?' your name comes up." After I got the job, becoming the first Black coach ever at a school in what is now known as the Power 5 conferences (ACC, Big Ten, Big 12, Pac-12, and the SEC), he said, "Coach, could I say one thing to you before you leave?"

"Yes, sir," I said.

"I'll always be there when you're losing," he said. "I'll never be there when you're winning."

I'll never forget that as long as I live.

He stayed true to his word. After three straight losing seasons to begin my head-coaching career, I got a call from my secretary to tell me that the athletic director wanted to meet with me that afternoon in his office. I hung up and then called my wife to let her know that I was probably about to get fired. When I walked into the AD's office, I sat down, and he said, "President Carroll and I have been talking about you a lot lately, and we decided that we're going to give you a three-year extension and a twenty-five-hundred-dollar raise."

I was stunned. I didn't know what the hell to say. And then he said, "Coach, just think about what we're going to do when you start winning." Their commitment to me was unwavering. The following season, we had the first of five straight winning seasons, making it to the NCAA tournament in 1980—the first time Washington State had been there in thirty-nine years—and in 1983.

This, to me, is the defining element of friendship. Everyone wants to be there for you when you're winning. Friends want to be there for you when you're losing.

It's in those losing moments that we find out who really listens, who truly cares about your struggles as much as they do your successes.

In my life, I've tried to be that person for others because so many have been that person for me. That's what I was trying to be for James when he called me. He didn't have to tell me something was wrong. I just knew. The art of listening, which we explored earlier, goes beyond words. It's about tuning in to what isn't being said, picking up on the unspoken signals. In that moment, I wasn't just hearing James's voice—I was hearing everything he wasn't able to say.

Friendships are built on that same kind of deep understanding, where you know your friend well enough to recognize when something is off or when they need someone by their side. One of my best friends, though, was Bobby Knight. We met for the first time in 1972, when we were both early in our coaching careers. I was doing some recruiting at a summer league game in Narberth, Pennsylvania, and after the game, I went to the scorekeeper's table to take a look at the score book. As I was looking it over, someone tapped me on the shoulder and asked, "Can I take a look at that?" I turned around and he stuck out his hand and introduced himself: "Bob Knight. I'm an assistant coach at West Point."

"George Raveling," I said. "Villanova."

Bob paused for a moment to look at the numbers, then asked, "Hey, is there a place around here to get a decent milkshake?"

I knew a spot up the street, and over milkshakes, we talked about everything from the players who stood out during the game that night to life on the recruiting circuit, coaching philosophies, and our goals and aspirations. At one point, he mentioned a recruit he was hoping they might land at West Point. I knew the player was already committed and pulled out my extensive list of prospects from all over the country, which I kept meticulously on accounting sheets. He was astonished and asked, "Where the hell did you get this list from?" "I read all the newspapers I can," I told him. There was a newsstand at Thirtieth and Market in Philly that carried out-of-town newspapers from most of the big cities in the U.S. I would go there and the owner would let me go through the sports pages.

Bob and I traded phone numbers and stayed in touch. I told you his advice earlier: "George, if you're going to survive in this profession, you have to become the foremost expert in some phase of the game." Not long after, he called me and said, "I got it. You're going to make yourself an expert in rebounding." The next day, he called again: "Hey, I looked it up in the Library of Congress—there's no book on rebounding, so you've got a unique opportunity. Write an outline and send it to me." That advice led me to write the book *War on the Boards*.

Our friendship wasn't always smooth sailing. Friendships, of course, aren't just about telling people what they want to hear all the time. Sometimes, you have to give them feedback and tough love. I had many tough conversations with Bob.

During the 1984 Olympics, there was a game in which one of our best players, Patrick Ewing, got off to a terrible start. Bob subbed him out and then publicly berated me. "It's your goddamn fault, Raveling," he said. "You took him out to dinner last night."

"Hey, Bob, fuck you," I said, and then I walked to the end of the bench and decided to let him fend for himself the rest of the game. As I said, friends have to be able to be straight with each other.

I think Bob knew he screwed up because in the third quarter, with the game not going well, the team manager, Tim Garl, came over to me and said, "George, you got to come back up. Coach Knight needs you."

I don't think I had consciously thought about it, but by this point, those words from the AD were instilled in me: "I'll always be there when you're losing." Friendships are forged by the heat of those times when tensions and emotions flare. I walked over and let Bob know I had his back. After the game, he apologized for being out of line. "Yeah, you were," I said. "Ewing and I didn't even get dinner together last night." Which was the truth. I don't know how he got that idea in his head. But we won the game together, laughed about the whole thing, and moved on, our friendship forged a little bit stronger by the heated exchange.

Bob was well-known for his fiery temper. And he had an intense, imposing demeanor that made him seem very intimidating. But over the years, I found a way to cut through all that. If I wanted to stop him in his tracks, I just had to say, "Hey, Coach, I just want you to know one thing. I love you, man. You changed my life."

That would melt him right down. As it does most people. I've learned that it's hard for people, especially males, to tell other people, "I love you." Even with my own son, for most of his early years, I noticed it was uncomfortable for him to say "I love you," back to me. It's strange because each and every one of us has a thirst to be loved, to be appreciated, acknowledged, respected. And yet, for some reason, there's a difficulty or discomfort in expressing to others, "I love you." "I appreciate you." "I respect you." "I'm glad you're my friend." "I know we have our differences, but I'm here for you."

I think we would be surprised by how few people regularly hear these kinds of things. I would wager that over half of the young people in America go to bed every night without having heard a single affirming word.

So I developed the habit of saying what people don't hear enough. At the end of every conversation with pretty much anyone who is not a complete stranger, I say two things. First, I ask sincerely, "Is there anything I can do for you?" And second, I tell them, "I love you."

We're social beings. We're made for each other. We're bees of the same hive, and like the honey that emerges from the harmony of the bees working together in their hive, we must take time to invest in our relationships.

One of the most valuable lessons I've learned about relationships is that you never know where life will take the people you meet. Over the years, I've been fortunate to build friendships with basically every major figure in basketball for all of the twentieth century: Wilt Chamberlain, Michael Jordan, Kobe Bryant, Jerry West, John Wooden, Bill Walton, Kareem Abdul-Jabbar, Charles Barkley, John Thompson, Chuck Daly—the list goes on.

But here's the thing: when I met many of these people, they weren't yet the legends they'd become.

Take Bill Walton, for example. I first met him when he was a lanky, injury-prone kid at Helix High School in San Diego. Back then, it wasn't obvious that he was going to be a superstar. As a sophomore, he played on the junior varsity team. When he moved up to varsity as a 6'7", 180-pound junior, he was gangly and only able to play limited minutes. By his senior year, he grew stronger and improved his conditioning, and that season, he averaged 29 points and 24 rebounds while leading Helix to a 33-0 record and a state championship.

I was coaching at Washington State at the time and tried to recruit him. At first, I thought I had a real shot at getting him. When I started recruiting him, he hadn't fully exploded onto the national radar. But as his senior year progressed, the odds of landing him began to slip away as the bigger programs started circling. Bill ultimately chose UCLA, where he led the Bruins to back-to-back 30-0 seasons and powered their legendary eighty-eight-game winning streak. He was named College Player of the Year three times, and many consider him the greatest college player ever.

Even after he chose UCLA, Bill and I stayed in touch. Over the years, we built a friendship, and he loved to tease me about my recruiting efforts, saying, "George, you had a lot of guts thinking you could get me to play at Washington State." That was part of Bill's charm—he was as playful as he was intense on the court. Our bond went beyond basketball. Bill was an intellectual, always diving into books, philosophy, and deep conversations about life. Our talks stretched far beyond the game, and that's what I appreciated most about him: his mind was constantly exploring, always curious and eager to learn.

As the years went by, our friendship grew stronger and stronger. And by the last year of his life, I felt like I was closer to Bill than ever. That's the thing with relationships—you never know where they'll take you or how they'll evolve. It never ceases to amaze me the way someone you meet as a high school recruit or a coaching peer can later become such a significant figure in your life. The same goes for the other greats I've known. I first met Wilt Chamberlain when he was a senior at Overbrook High School in West Philadelphia, playing on the local playgrounds. And Kobe, when he was a high school student at Lower Merion, just outside Philly.

Back then, they were simply people I met along the way, strangers who crossed paths, the way we often do in life. These were just chance encounters, ordinary moments that turned into extraordinary relationships over time. I had no way of knowing that these individuals would go on to become some of the most influential figures in basketball history. I was simply interested in connecting with people, learning from them, and helping where I could.

You never know who someone will become or how your paths will continue to cross. It's a reminder to stay open to people, to connect sincerely, because some of those relationships will become the ones that shape your life in ways you can't yet imagine.

I think about this often—when Barack Obama was at Occidental College, he couldn't get a roommate. Nobody wanted to room with this skinny Black kid with a funny name. Imagine being one of his classmates who overlooked him—now looking back and realizing they turned down the chance to get to know someone who would become the president of the United States.

The point isn't the missed opportunity to befriend a future president—it's a reminder that every person we meet has value, regardless of who they might become.

Relationships are built not on who people are, but on how we treat them. You don't wait for someone to achieve success before showing them respect or kindness. You build those connections through genuine interest, through being present in the moment with them. It's about investing in relationships for the sake of the relationship, for the shared humanity. You never know where those connections will take you—or where they'll take the other person.

It's like one of the things I tell young college coaches when they come to me for advice when they land their first head-coaching job. I always tell them to make sure they start a meaningful relationship with the athletic director. An AD tends to have a lot of out-of-balance relationships, giving more than they get. Head coaches are so focused on their job, which is great, but it means that most of them aren't going out of their way to do anything for their AD. So I tell the people who come to me: "Sometime in the first few weeks, call the AD and ask for a short meeting. And when you meet, say to them, 'I guess you're wondering why I asked to meet with you. I just wanted to find out more about your job as the AD so I can learn how I can help you.' They'll be stunned."

It's good policy—and not just if you're in college athletics—to have meaningful relationships with the people who can get you fired. If someone has even a pinky on the steering wheel of your career and life, make sure you have a meaningful relationship with that person.

It's not just about self-interest or self-preservation.

It's about being a decent, thoughtful, good human being.

It's about being, instead of a leech, a contributing member of the hive.

It's about fulfilling a fundamental part of the purpose of a social being on this earth.

If you do that—if you fulfill your social duty, if you do what you were made for—I promise that you too will eventually be asked, "How do you account for all the great things that have happened to you in your life?"

And you will use one word to capture it all:

"Relationships."

To Build
Your Team

My most brilliant achievement was my ability to
be able to persuade my wife to marry me.

—WINSTON CHURCHILL

In the game of life, the most important team we'll ever be a part of is our family. Throughout my journey, I've come to see family not just as a group connected by blood or law, but as a team—a unit where each member plays a crucial role in our collective success and well-being.

At the helm of Team Raveling is my wife, Delores, the CEO of our family. We met in 1988 through a mutual friend while she was pursuing her doctorate at USC. Her academic journey is impressive—from Illinois State for her undergraduate studies to a master's at UCLA, and finally her doctorate at USC. When we met, there was an immediate connection. Our relationship grew into a strong partnership that led to marriage in 1995.

When I reflect on my life, one thing stands out: I could never have achieved what I have without my wife by my side. She has been my unwavering rock, offering steadfast support, wisdom, and guidance every step of the way. But her role extends far beyond supporting the family—she's the one who keeps everything running smoothly, making decisions that benefit all of us and ensuring our lives remain balanced.

She's not just the CEO of our family; she's also my truth-teller. When it comes to being honest with me, she never hesitates. She's the first to offer an unfiltered perspective, especially when it's something I need to hear, even if it's not what I want to hear. For instance, when I receive awards or public recognition, she doesn't just offer congratulations and move on—she makes a deliberate effort to keep me grounded. There's an old, offensive line—more popular in my day—where men would refer to their wives as "the old ball and chain." I would never say that, but you know what? Delores has kept me anchored. She's kept my feet on ground. Kept me from falling off.

It's not that she doesn't appreciate my achievements; in fact, she's incredibly proud of them. But she also understands how easily success can inflate one's ego. She's there to remind me that while accolades are fleeting, humility and integrity are what truly endure.

A marriage, much like any meaningful relationship, requires more than just mutual respect and support—it demands forgiveness. I'm reminded of a modern trend that Arthur Ashe, the legendary tennis player and a pioneer both on and off the court, reflected on in his memoir, *Days of Grace*, which he wrote in part for the daughter he would not be able to see grow up. "Nowadays," Ashe writes, "people break up marriages over the slightest of differences, which is a pity." On the night before Ashe's wedding, a close confidant gave him and his bride some sage advice, emphasizing that the most important ingredient in a marriage is forgiveness—the willingness of each partner to forgive the other.

Forgiving takes courage, but it is the key. As Ashe noted, "No marriage or truly important human relationship can survive, let alone flourish, without both partners willing to forgive."

Ashe married his wife, Jeanne Moutoussamy-Ashe, in 1977, and they remained together until his passing in 1993. Their union endured for sixteen years, weathering both triumphs and trials, including Ashe's public battle with AIDS. His reflections on marriage are not just the words of a tennis legend, but of a man who understood the depth and complexity of relationships. Over the years, Delores and I have had to lean on that advice. It's a reminder that while our roles and responsibilities may change, the underlying principles that hold us together—like forgiveness—remain constant.

In a relationship, it's easy to focus on what's wrong, to let minor disagreements fester into major conflicts. But the real strength lies in being able to see past those differences, to forgive, and to move forward together. Delores and I have always made it a point to work through our disagreements, to forgive quickly, and to keep moving forward. It's not always easy, but it's what has kept our marriage strong through the years.

When I look at the landscape of marriages today, I see too many relationships breaking apart over minor differences (and I say that with sympathy, not judgment; this is my second marriage, after all). It's a trend that saddens me, because I know that with a bit more forgiveness, more marriages could flourish. In our family, we've learned that it's not about keeping score or holding on to grudges; it's about letting go, forgiving, and focusing on the love that brought us together in the first place.

Forgiveness, resilience, and the willingness to move forward—these are the cornerstones not just of a strong marriage, but of any strong team. And when it comes to building a family, these qualities are essential. Without them, the foundation cracks and the team falters. But with them, anything is possible.

As I said, a spouse keeps you tethered to reality, especially when you're in roles that expose you to constant praise and adulation. This grounding influence extends to my children as well. My daughter, Litisha, my son, Mark, and my stepdaughter, Marissa, have all been integral parts of Team Raveling, each bringing their unique strengths and perspectives to our family dynamic. They have always helped me by setting boundaries, reminding me of my responsibilities and obligations, ensuring I never lose touch with what's real and important and, of course, embodying the ideas of love and connection.

Litisha has always embodied the dedication and hard work we value as a family. After earning her undergraduate degree from San Diego State and a master's from Long Beach State, she went on to work at Nike, where she served as my administrative assistant for over twenty years. Her role was far more than just an assistant; Litisha became an essential part of my professional life, helping me navigate the corporate world with her insight and diligence.

Watching Litisha grow into a savvy, capable professional while maintaining the warmth and compassion that define her as a person has been a source of immense pride for me. Her journey from daughter to professional partner has been one of the most rewarding experiences of my life.

My son, Mark, has also thrived at Nike, rising to become the director of player relations for Jordan Brand and later serving as my financial adviser. And Marissa has been a cherished part of my life since I married Delores. Their achievements fill me with pride, but more important, they keep me connected to the values of diligence and integrity that have always guided our family. It was Mark, ultimately, who helped get the wheels turning on this book—an activity I have enjoyed so much.

The bond I share with my children has evolved over time, shaped by the experiences we've had together. When Mark was younger, we would spend our summers together, traveling from basketball camps to speaking engagements. These summers weren't just about basketball or work; they were about the quiet moments in between. Whether it was grabbing sandwiches in small-town delis, sitting in hotel rooms, or just hanging out and talking, those were the times when we truly connected, not just as father and son, but as friends.

I never pushed basketball on Mark, just as I never pushed Litisha toward any particular career path. It wasn't until junior high school that Mark really got into the sport. But when he asked me to go to the gym and work with him, I was always happy to do so. I tried to strike a balance between being supportive and not being overbearing. Similarly, when Litisha expressed interest in business and management, I encouraged her pursuits while allowing her to forge her own path.

However, balancing a demanding career with fatherhood wasn't always easy. When I took the USC job, Mark moved to Los Angeles for his junior and senior high school years. My coaching schedule often meant that I wasn't home as much as I would have liked. There were times it felt like we were roommates passing each other in the night. I'd go to bed early because of six a.m. practices, and by the time he woke up, I was already gone. Road trips would take me away from Wednesday to Sunday or Monday.

We say that we're "doing it all for them," but are we? My father lived away from us because it was the only way to make a living. Dear was gone because she was working more jobs than I can remember. But me? It was a choice . . . and in some ways that made it harder.

Children have a remarkable way of pulling you back to reality, often with blunt honesty. For example, if I've promised to take them to the zoo and something significant comes up, they're quick to remind me that a promise is a promise. To them, it doesn't matter who I am or what my role is—what matters is that I keep my word. That kind of accountability is both refreshing and essential, anchoring me to the real world, where my responsibilities to those I love come first, no matter what's happening in my professional life.

But it's not just about keeping promises; it's about being fully present when you are with your family. In a world where work often demands more than a fifty-fifty split, it's easy to let the pressures of the job encroach on the time you spend at home. I quickly realized that achieving a perfect work-life balance wasn't always possible. Instead, I had to make deliberate choices to be fully engaged when I was with my family. When I was home with Delores and the kids, I made it a point to focus on them, to be there in the moment, because that's what really matters.

Mark and Litisha didn't care that I was a successful basketball coach. What mattered to them was whether I said yes when they asked me to go to the gym, or if I kept my promise to take them to the zoo. Those moments—those simple, everyday interactions—are the building blocks of a legacy at home. Just as I worked hard to build a professional legacy, I knew I had to invest as much, if not more, in building a legacy within my own home. And that begins with being present—truly present—when you're with your family.

In striving to build a career and a legacy, we sometimes miss out on the day-to-day moments that matter most. But by making the conscious choice to be present, to prioritize the people we love when we're with them, we ensure that the legacy we leave behind is one of love, support, and connection—both at work and at home.

One of the rarest and most profound moments in life is hearing your child describe being deeply in touch with their emotions and expressing genuine pride in you. I vividly recall when my son Mark shared a story with me years after the 1992 NCAA tournament. We had lost a heartbreaking game to Georgia Tech on a last-second half-court shot. Mark, watching the game alone at home, told me he broke down in tears. He said he knew how much that game meant to me and to the team. That kind of empathy—the ability to feel another's joy or sorrow as your own—is something truly special. What he didn't know is that hearing him tell me this story, knowing how deeply he felt for us, is worth as much as any trophy.

The strength of Team Raveling extends beyond our immediate family. We are fortunate to have an extended team that plays a significant role in our collective success. Kimati Ramsey, my trusted business partner, and Daniel Chu, my personal consultant, are both vital members of this team. I communicate with each of them almost daily—sometimes, with Kimati, up to five times a day. These individuals are the lifeblood of Team Raveling, each contributing in their unique way to our shared goals and success.

When you commit to a relationship, you're making a decision to accept both the best and the worst aspects of the other person. But it doesn't stop there. When you enter into that relationship, you also inherit all of the other person's relationships, both positive and challenging. This expansion of your network, or what I like to call your "relationship tree," can be enriching and complex. It's through this relationship tree that we grow not only as individuals but as a collective unit. The branches of our lives intertwine, offering new opportunities for connection, support, and growth. But they also bring new challenges that require patience, understanding, and communication. The strength of a team, especially a family, lies in its ability to navigate these complexities together, supporting one another through the highs and lows.

People talk about their personal life and their professional life as if they are two separate entities. But the fact of the matter is that we only have one life. It's all connected, whether we want to admit it or not. How we live our lives at home affects how we show up at work. The quality of our work life affects how we are as a spouse and a parent. So, I tried to live an integrated life as much as possible.

This wasn't always easy, especially in a profession as demanding as coaching, but I found ways to make it work. My family was never just on the sidelines; they were part of the game, holding me accountable, cheering for me, and at times crying alongside me. When I was on the road, my thoughts often drifted to my wife and kids, knowing that whatever success I achieved on the court would mean little if I failed them at home. This understanding shaped my decisions, guided my actions, and kept me grounded.

It's worth noting that there are many great coaches, athletes, business leaders, and even world leaders who are so focused on changing the world and making an impact on others that they often neglect the most important impact—the one on their own family. They might be influencing thousands or even millions of people, but what about their children, their spouse, or their grandchildren?

These are the people who matter most, and the impact you have on them is far more significant than any public achievement.

One of the things I've always valued in my relationship with Mark is the way it has evolved over time. As he grew older and began his career at Nike and Jordan Brand, we found new ways to connect. We had more to talk about—business, leadership, challenges we both faced in our respective roles. It was a natural progression from the summers we spent together when he was younger to the partnership we developed running the Jordan Flight School basketball camp. Trust is the foundation of any relationship, and there came a time when I knew I could trust Mark to take the lead. Handing him the responsibility of running the camp wasn't just about delegation—it was about acknowledging his growth, his capabilities, and the man he had become. Watching him manage those camps with the same care and dedication I had always put into them was one of my proudest moments as a father.

When we talk about building a team, this doesn't necessarily mean you have to get married or have children, but it does mean that you can't go through life alone. No one can be an island unto themselves. Success in any endeavor, whether personal or professional, requires a support system. You need to surround yourself with people who uplift you, challenge you, and help you grow. The notion of a "self-made" person is a myth. Success is never achieved in isolation. Each of us is the sum of our surroundings—the influences, environments, family, and friends that shape us. Behind every successful individual is a network of people who have supported, guided, and uplifted them at every turn.

This is why I believe that more families could benefit from clearly defining each member's role and openly discussing these roles. How many families actually sit down together and ask, "How can we be a better family? How can we be more productive? How can we help each other live better lives?" These are crucial questions that often go unasked. Just because a family lives under the same roof doesn't mean they're living better lives together. It takes deliberate effort, communication, and a shared commitment to improve the quality of life for everyone in the household.

In the end, we are a reflection of the support and guidance we receive from the countless individuals who shape our lives. Our achievements are not isolated milestones but rather the culmination of relationships, environments, and communities that nurture us. By acknowledging this, we can appreciate the true nature of success—not as a solitary pursuit, but as a shared journey.

When I look back on my life, it's clear that we are all part of something greater than ourselves. We are links in a chain, connected to those who came before us and those who will follow. My grandmother, Dear, profoundly shaped me with her wisdom and love. Now, as a grandparent, I hope to have even a fraction of that impact on my grandchildren.

This web of relationships and influences isn't just a metaphor—it's the essence of what makes us human. We are social beings, designed to live, work, and thrive within a community. Our greatest joys, deepest sorrows, and most significant achievements gain meaning through our connections with others.

As you contemplate your own path, remember this: You were made for connection. You were made to be part of a team—whether it's a family by blood, a family by choice, or both. You were made to support and be supported, to love and be loved, to challenge and be challenged.

You were made to build a team that lifts you up, celebrates

your victories, and helps you become the best version of yourself. A team that keeps you grounded and helps you navigate life's complexities.

You were made to be part of something bigger than yourself—a family, a community, a legacy that extends beyond your individual achievements.

So, build your team.

Nurture your relationships.

Embrace the richness of human connection.

Because in the end, that's what we were made for—to build and be part of a team that makes life richer, more meaningful, and profoundly rewarding.

To Tell
the Truth

Beauty is truth, truth beauty,—that is all
Ye know on earth, and all ye need to know.

—JOHN KEATS

In April 1984, the Olympic basketball trials were held in Bloomington, Indiana, on the campus of Indiana University. It was perhaps the greatest collection of collegiate talent ever assembled in one place. The very best college basketball players in America were vying for spots on the team that would represent the United States at the upcoming Summer Olympics in Los Angeles.

As an assistant coach on Bob Knight's staff, I found myself in the thick of it all. We put the players through drills and scrimmages, gradually whittling down the pool of candidates. The talent was extraordinary, with several future Hall of Famers among the hopefuls.

During a crucial staff meeting to discuss our final selections, Bob Knight, the head coach, turned to us assistants—me, Don Donoher from Dayton, and C. M. Newton from Vanderbilt.

"Okay," he said, "each one of you go up and write down the fifteen players you'd keep on the team."

When we finished, I noticed that all three of us had included Charles Barkley on our lists. Bob looked at our selections and exploded, "Damn, maybe I hired the wrong staff. You guys don't know what the hell you're talking about. Barkley is not going to be on this team."

We argued vigorously for Charles's inclusion, but Bob was adamant. "Charles will not accept coaching," he insisted. "I want to remind you, we're not picking an all-star team. We're picking a team to win the gold medal. I'm not going to waste time trying to coach Charles."

After emotions subsided and we agreed to reconvene later, Bob pulled me aside.

"George, you stay here," he said after the others had left. "You go tell Barkley that he's cut."

This is one of the most challenging aspects of leadership: the need to deliver hard truths directly and compassionately. Many leaders struggle with this, often skirting issues or deflecting blame to avoid confrontation. They make up stories in their heads about how negatively the person might react to feedback or bad news, and this anxiety can lead to a failure of honest communication.

As Kim Scott writes in her book *Radical Candor*, "When you are overly worried about how people will perceive you, you're less willing to say what needs to be said." This reluctance to be forthright can have serious consequences. It can leave people in the dark about their performance, stifle growth and improvement, and erode trust within a team or organization.

Facing Barkley in that moment, I knew I had to embody the kind of leadership I believed in—one based on honesty and respect. I couldn't BS him and I had to deliver the news straight. (Is there anything worse than when someone sugarcoats something so much you're not actually sure where you stand?) It wasn't easy, but I understood that my discomfort was far less important than Charles's right to know the truth and move forward with clarity. I've learned that in sports: You gotta sit the player down and tell them they're cut or they're being traded or they're not ready. No dancing around it. No stringing them along.

It was a difficult task, but I found Charles and delivered the news. To my surprise, he handled it with remarkable grace. "You know I should be on this team," he said. "But honestly, I accomplished what I wanted to accomplish. I wanted the NBA scouts to see that I can play against any of these guys."

I respected Charles's honesty—not with me, but with himself. He had a clear understanding of why he was there and what he wanted to achieve. This kind of introspection and clear-eyed realism is rare. It's easy to lie to ourselves about our motivation, to get caught up in the chase for accolades and job titles and bragging rights, to tell ourselves we're aiming for one thing when we're really driven by something else entirely. It's easy to let the status signals of making an Olympic team or getting a certain job title disconnect us from what we truly desire.

Charles knew his path, and he stayed true to it. He didn't need an Olympic gold medal to validate his worth or his talent. Instead, he focused on the next steps in his career. That clarity paid off. Just a few months later, he was selected as the fifth overall pick in the 1984 NBA draft by the Philadelphia 76ers, where he quickly established himself as one of the most dominant power forwards the game has ever seen. Over his sixteen-year NBA career, Charles would become an eleven-time NBA All-Star, an

NBA MVP, and one of the 50 Greatest Players in NBA History. He was later inducted into the Naismith Memorial Basketball Hall of Fame, not once but twice—first as a player and then as a member of the "Dream Team" that won gold at the 1992 Olympics.

Charles's success wasn't just about his physical abilities, which were formidable. It was about his unwavering self-awareness and confidence in who he was and what he could achieve. He understood that true greatness comes not from chasing every accolade, but from knowing your strengths, owning your weaknesses, and pursuing your goals with relentless determination. Charles didn't make the 1984 Olympic team, but he went on to build a legacy that few could rival, proving that sometimes, not getting what you want can lead you exactly where you need to be.

Not just in how he handled getting cut, but in how he handles himself all the time, Charles helped me realize that telling the truth isn't just about making grand declarations or coming clean with others. Being a truth-teller starts as an inside job. It starts at home. It's about the honesty we maintain with ourselves in the little silences throughout our life. It's about being true and authentic in our pursuits, our motivations, our desires. Because if we can't tell ourselves the truth, how can we be truthful with anyone else?

This wouldn't be the only time Charles's straightforward honesty would leave an impression on me. Years later, it would surface in an unexpected and humorous way, tied to another significant moment in my life.

As I mentioned earlier, I had the privilege of standing alongside Dr. Martin Luther King Jr. on the steps of the Lincoln Memorial during the March on Washington. After Dr. King delivered his historic "I Have a Dream" speech, he handed me his typewritten notes, which I've preserved ever since.

Over the years, many people have tried to buy the speech from me. One collector even offered $3.5 million. But I never felt that the speech was mine to sell. I saw myself as the guardian of a historic artifact, not its owner.

Charles, in his characteristic blunt and humorous style, addressed this in a documentary about my life. He joked, "I've offered him millions of dollars for that speech. . . . I've actually thought about just beating the hell out of him one day and taking the speech, but I got so much love and respect for him."

Charles's comment, while funny, speaks to his nature as a truth-teller. He didn't hide his desire for the speech, nor did he shy away from expressing his respect for me. It's this kind of candid honesty, even in jest, that makes Charles such a compelling figure.

It was also a way of delivering an important truth to me: I had to figure out what I was going to do with the speech and how its ownership would be handled in the future. It was too much responsibility and meant too much to just belong to one man.

In 2021, I decided to donate the papers to my alma mater, Villanova, choosing them as the permanent steward. To ensure the broadest possible exposure for Dr. King's powerful message, Villanova will loan the document to museums and institutions around the world. When not on loan, the speech resides on Villanova's campus.

This decision, I believe, honors the truth of what the speech represents. It's not a personal possession to be sold to the highest bidder, but a piece of our shared history that should be preserved and shared with as many people as possible.

As I continued my coaching career, I often thought back to that conversation with Charles. It became a touchstone for me. I would ask players, "Are you being honest with yourself about why you're here? Are you clear on what you want to achieve?" And I began to see how the ability or inability to tell the truth deeply and fundamentally determines the path a person takes in life. How it shapes not just individual moments, but a person's entire life. How little lies and self-deceptions compound over time, leading people into professions that ultimately leave them unfulfilled and disconnected from their true desires.

On the other hand, I've seen the power of honesty, both with oneself and with others. I've seen how people who are unafraid to authentically pursue their path, people who confront hard truths, people who are willing to have difficult conversations and make tough choices in alignment with their deepest values tend to lead lives of authenticity and purpose.

This doesn't mean that telling the truth is always easy or comfortable. More often than not, it's the opposite. It requires facing difficult realities, risking disappointment, and sometimes being misunderstood. But true growth and progress come from these moments of discomfort. Whether it's cutting a player from a team or turning down an opportunity that doesn't align with your values, truth-telling is often a solitary road—but it's a necessary one.

Over the years, I've had to deliver plenty of hard truths as a coach and mentor. I've had to tell players that they weren't ready for the NBA or that their attitude was affecting the entire team. Those conversations were never easy, but they were essential. The most caring thing you can do for someone is to tell them the truth, even when it's not the truth they want to hear.

And sometimes, the hard truth isn't just about telling someone what they don't want to hear—it's about revealing what others don't want you to share. During the 1975 season, when I was coaching at Washington State, I wrote a weekly column that was syndicated in the local newspapers, including *The Seattle Times* and *The Spokesman-Review*. I was talking to my good friend Gene Bartow, who told me he had just signed a contract to replace John Wooden as head coach at UCLA. I remember telling him, "Damn, you know it's going to be tough as hell following a legend. The only thing they expect there is a national championship."

This was big news in the coaching world, news that UCLA was playing very coy about. I'm not a big fan of "open secrets," so I decided I would write about it. I asked Gene if that would be OK, and he said yes, as long as I kept the source to myself.

As you can imagine, all hell broke loose when the column hit the presses. The UCLA athletic director was furious. He thought he could stage-manage the whole process and was livid I had destroyed their polite fictions. I believed people deserved to know the truth, and that it was a significant moment in college basketball history.

The AD threatened me, trying to smoke out my sources. The Pac-8 commissioner even suspended me temporarily because of it. But as they say, the truth is always the best defense.

That's not to say that telling the truth is free! Today, people talk about free speech, but there have *always* been consequences for what we do and say. Whether it's anger from those in power, hurt feelings, or public controversy, the fallout from truth-telling is real.

You gotta be tough enough to handle it.

But that cost is always worth it when you stand by what's right, no matter how uncomfortable or inconvenient it may be.

As you read this, I invite you to reflect on your own relationship with truth:

Would you want someone to tell you the truth about your presentation if it didn't land?

Would you want someone to tell you the truth about your leadership skills if they were failing to achieve results?

Would you rather someone tell you the truth or let you lie to yourself?

How would your life be different if everyone in it committed to telling you the hard truths you need to hear?

These aren't easy questions to answer, but they're crucial ones. Our willingness to hear and tell the truth shapes not just our individual interactions, but the entire trajectory of our lives and careers.

This is something coaches have to wrestle with constantly.

During my time at Nike, I saw how a commitment to honesty and transparency could transform a company from the inside out.

Phil Knight, the cofounder and former CEO of Nike, was one of the most honest and authentic leaders I've ever known. In all my years working with him, I never once knew him to tell a lie. His word was his bond, and you could count on him to shoot straight no matter what. That integrity trickled down through every level of the organization. It became a core part of the Nike culture—this idea that we would succeed or fail on the strength of our ideas and the truth of our intentions, not on spin or politics or empty hype. This culture of honesty and authenticity, combined with the company's innovative spirit and commitment to excellence, made Nike the best place in the world to work. It was an environment where truth-telling wasn't just encouraged—it was expected and rewarded.

That commitment to truth-telling paid off in concrete ways. It allowed us to confront challenges head-on, to have the difficult conversations that needed to be had in order to find real solutions. It gave us the clarity of vision to make bold moves, like investing in new technologies and markets before our competitors. And it earned us the trust of our customers and partners, who knew that we would always strive to do the right thing, even when it wasn't the easy thing.

The value of truth-telling in leadership was further reinforced for me through an unexpected opportunity with the Los Angeles Clippers. I remember a conversation I had with Doc Rivers that really brought this idea of responsibility into focus. Doc called me out of the blue one day and asked if I wanted to go to lunch. I said sure, not knowing what he had in mind. Over lunch, he asked me if I'd be interested in becoming a consultant for the Clippers. I asked him to tell me more about it, and he explained what he had in mind. After listening to his vision, I agreed, and I've been a consultant for the Clippers ever since.

A few months into the job, I went to Doc's office and asked him, "What are your expectations? Why did you pick me for this role?" He looked me straight in the eye and said, "I need somebody who's going to tell me the truth. People around here might hold things back or tell me what they think I want to hear. But I need someone who's going to be honest with me, whether I'm going to like it or not. I respect your judgment. You're one of the most respected guys in coaching, and I need someone who will tell me the truth."

That conversation stuck with me because it reinforced what I've always believed: that our role, especially as we get older, is to help others by being honest, by sharing what we've learned, and by paying it forward.

Doc's request for honesty speaks volumes about the rarity and value of truth-tellers in any organization. In a world where people often prioritize pleasing their superiors over speaking hard truths, Doc recognized the vital importance of having someone who would give him unvarnished feedback.

And this is true at every level of leadership. The story "The Emperor's New Clothes" is a timeless reminder of what happens when leaders are surrounded by sycophants and flatterers. In modern political science, they call this the "dictator's knowledge problem." The tyrant needs information to survive, but people are afraid to give them bad news, so they come to live in their own bubble of delusion and partial truth, which only worsens as the situation around them worsens.

Truth-telling isn't just a personal virtue—it's a professional asset. In fact, it's one of the most valuable things we can offer as mentors, consultants, and leaders. Our willingness to speak truth to power, to offer honest feedback even when it's uncomfortable, can be the difference between an organization that stagnates and one that continually improves and innovates.

Moreover, Doc's approach demonstrates the kind of leadership that fosters a culture of honesty. By actively seeking out truth-tellers and valuing their input, he was setting a tone for the entire organization. He was saying, in effect, that the Clippers were a team that prioritized truth over comfort, growth over complacency.

Whether in sports or business, the most effective leaders are those who not only tell the truth themselves but also surround themselves with people who will tell them the truth. They understand that honest feedback, even when it's critical, is a gift that helps them grow and improve.

Of course, even for a truth-telling culture like Nike's, honesty doesn't always mean full transparency. There are times when certain truths need to be kept close to the vest, when decisions need to be made without a public paper trail. I've been in plenty of high-level meetings that ended with the directive: "There is to be no email trail on this."

The key is to be intentional and discerning about when and how the truth gets told. To understand that sometimes the most effective way to drive change is not through a megaphone, but through quiet, strategic action behind the scenes. To balance the courage of your convictions with the wisdom to know when to speak and when to keep counsel.

This is the art of truth-telling, and it's something that the best leaders and change-makers understand intuitively. They know that honesty is not just about what you say in the public square, but about how you move in the world, how you build consensus and create coalitions, how you navigate the complex dance of competing interests and shifting alliances.

At its core, the art of truth-telling is about aligning your words and your actions, your values and your deeds. It's about having the strength of character to show up as your authentic self in every context, to speak and live in alignment with your deepest convictions.

It's not an easy path. It requires constant self-reflection, a willingness to question your own beliefs and assumptions, a commitment to growth and learning. It means being open to the truth, even when it's uncomfortable or inconvenient or challenges your cherished ideas about yourself and the world.

But in my experience, it's the only path worth walking. Because a life lived in truth is a life of integrity, of wholeness, of deep and abiding purpose. It's a life that honors the best of what we're made for—to be beacons of honesty in a world that is hungry for authenticity and meaning.

As I look back on my journey, I see that telling the truth has been the through line that connects all the disparate chapters—from the hard lessons learned on the streets of Chocolate City to the Hall of Fame moments on the basketball court to the boardroom battles at Nike. In every arena, the commitment to honesty has been the compass that kept me true, the foundation upon which everything else was built.

And now, in the autumn of my life, I see that truth-telling isn't just a personal ethic, but a sacred duty. It's the obligation we have to each other and to the generations that will come after us—to leave this world a little bit better, a little bit truer than we found it.

That's the charge I hope to pass on to all those I have the privilege of mentoring and influencing. To be truth-tellers in a world that is often afraid of the truth. To have the courage to speak honestly, even when it's hard. To have the humility to listen deeply, even when it challenges your assumptions. To have the integrity to live your truth, even when it means standing alone.

This is how we build a world that is worthy of our highest ideals and aspirations. One conversation, one decision, one truth at a time.

So let honesty be your North Star. In every interaction, every decision, every moment, let us ask ourselves: Am I being true? Am I aligning my words and my actions with my deepest values and beliefs? Am I using my voice and my influence to champion honesty, authenticity, and integrity?

The answers won't always be easy or clear-cut. But if we stay the course, if we keep orienting ourselves toward the truth, we will become the kind of people, the kind of leaders, the kind of society that we know we can be. We will build a world that is more honest, more authentic, more alive with possibility and potential.

That is the world we were made for. That is the world that truth-telling can create.

So let us go forth with courage and conviction, armed with the knowledge that every time we speak and live in truth, we are fulfilling our highest calling and purpose.

We were made to tell the truth. We can't do what we were made to do if we don't become who we were made to be.

To Win
the Day

The will to win—I'm not sure I've ever seen a competitive athlete that doesn't want to win. The will to *prepare* to win is so much more important than the will to win.

—COACH BOBBY KNIGHT

When Michael Jordan first approached me about running his basketball camps, I was hesitant. I had my doubts about his level of commitment. "Let me think about it," I told him.

Michael looked at me, puzzled. "What's there to think about?" he asked.

I looked him straight in the eye. "Are you going to be there every day? I'm not going to cheat the kids."

One of the reasons Michael and I got along is that I told him the truth and he did the same with me. Without missing a beat, he replied, "Coach, I tell you, I'm not doing this for money. If we do this, I'm going to be at the camp every day."

And true to his word, over the twenty-two years that we ran those camps together, Michael was there every day. His focus wasn't just on showing up for a photo op or slapping his name on the program. This wasn't some celebrity cashing in on his fame—Michael was fully committed, and that's what made the camps so special.

He didn't just make appearances. He was out there on the court playing pickup games with the campers, talking trash like it was an NBA game, and pushing them to compete. He gave advice, shared insights, and stayed connected with everyone. Michael's presence and dedication were what set those camps apart from anything else out there.

The success of the camps exceeded anything I could have imagined. And that was because of the way Michael showed up every day. He was there not to cash a check but to share what made him great: his relentless drive, his focus, and his passion for the game. That's what the campers took with them, and that's why the camp ran for over two decades.

Michael's approach to these camps reflects what it truly means to win the day. For him, winning wasn't just about big moments on the court—it was about showing up every day, fully committed to excellence. Whether it was a championship game or a youth camp, Michael treated everything with the same mindset.

He once told me, "Each time you win, it takes away a little of that hunger. The challenge is finding that same place in your mind—five, six, seven, eight times. That's hard." He added, "When people say winning the first championship is the hardest, I tell them, 'No, the next one is.' Because you're battling yourself, the monotony of doing the same things over and over. Most days, the battle is just with myself. Can I keep challenging myself? That's the hardest part."

That's what winning the day means. It's not about a single victory or a big moment—it's about showing up, doing the work, and making those small, daily choices that add up to something great over time. That's how Michael approached life, and it's why those camps—and everything else he touched—were so successful.

Winning the day isn't about grand strategies or long-term plans. It's about what you do today, right now, to be better than you were yesterday.

The true test of greatness isn't just in achieving success but in sustaining it. It's in finding ways to keep pushing yourself, to keep growing and evolving, even when you've reached the mountain-top. This is what "winning the day" is all about—embracing the daily grind, the small, often monotonous tasks, with the understanding that these are the building blocks of long-term success.

This insight from Michael Jordan perfectly encapsulates the idea of winning the day. It's not about one-off victories or achieving something great in a single moment; it's about the consistent, intentional actions you take every day to move closer to your goals. It's about the small victories, the daily habits, and the moment-to-moment choices that, when compounded over time, lead to extraordinary results.

When people talk about greatness in sports, they often focus on singular, heroic moments. One such moment that comes to mind is Michael Jordan's famous "flu game" in the 1997 NBA Finals.

It was June 11, 1997, Game 5 of the NBA Finals between the Chicago Bulls and Utah Jazz. The series was tied 2-2. Jordan had been up all night, violently ill. The exact cause of his illness has been the subject of much speculation over the years. Some accounts suggest it was the flu, others point to food poisoning from a late-night pizza, and some speculate it might have been altitude sickness. Whatever the cause, the result was clear: Jordan was in bad shape.

Around eight a.m., the team's trainer, Chip Schaefer, found Jordan curled up in the fetal position, wrapped in blankets, with the thermostat cranked as high as it would go. Jordan had missed breakfast with his teammates and was in no condition to join the pregame shoot-around. Schaefer immediately hooked him up to an IV, trying to get as much fluid into him as possible.

Was it food poisoning? Altitude sickness? The flu? No one knew for sure, but everyone who saw him thought the same thing: There's no way he's playing in Game 5. Jordan's mother, Deloris, even suggested he not play. "Mom," he replied, "I have to play." Jordan showed up at the Delta Center in Salt Lake City and told his coach he wanted to play.

What followed was the stuff of legend. Despite being visibly weakened, often doubled over on the court gasping for breath, Jordan led a comeback from a 16-point deficit in the first quarter. He exploded for 38 points, including 15 in the fourth quarter, securing a crucial win for the Bulls.

When people recount this story, they often talk about how Jordan tapped into something that the sports world still struggles to put into words. They focus on what he did that night, willing himself to greatness in those forty-eight minutes. They highlight the dramatic lead-up to the game—how Jordan spent the day bedridden, hooked to IVs, and constantly sipping Gatorade to stay hydrated, as if these last-minute interventions were the most impressive and rare elements of his performance.

But of course, the real key wasn't what happened on June 11, 1997. It was everything that came before—those moments of discipline, dedication, and drive that were unseen and uncelebrated. It was the countless hours spent honing his skills in the gym, the rigorous training that pushed him to his limits day after day. It was the meticulous study of game film, the precision with which he managed his diet and recovery, and the relentless pursuit of improvement in every facet of his game. That night was the culmination of years spent winning the day, over and over again.

This is what I always tried to impress upon the players I coached. Greatness isn't about rising to one extraordinary occasion—it's the product of countless ordinary ones. It's not the dramatic moments that define you, but the habits you've built when no one is watching. It's the quiet commitment to excellence, the relentless effort to win every day, that ultimately lead to greatness when the spotlight finally shines.

Kobe Bryant echoed this idea in *The Mamba Mentality*, writing, "You have to work hard in the dark to shine in the light. Meaning: It takes a lot of work to be successful, and people will celebrate that success, will celebrate that flash and hype. Behind that hype, though, is dedication, focus, and seriousness—all of which outsiders will never see."

The moments of glory, the championships, the accolades—these are what the world sees and celebrates. But these moments are merely the visible results of countless hours of unseen effort. It's the early-morning workouts, the late-night study sessions, the relentless pursuit of improvement in every aspect of your craft—these are the true building blocks of success.

These lessons from Michael and Kobe aren't about basketball. They're about life. They're about the power of clarity and consistency in achieving lasting success, in winning the day, every day. In any field, the people who truly excel are those who commit to excellence in their daily habits, who push themselves to grow and improve even when—especially when—no one else is watching. They understand that true success isn't about sporadic bursts of brilliance, but about consistent, dedicated effort over time.

For me, that starts with a simple but powerful choice every morning. As I put my feet on the floor, I say to myself, "Okay, George, you have two options today, and only two. You can be happy, or you can be very happy." It's a reminder to myself that I have the power to set the tone for my day, to choose the attitude and mindset that I'll bring to whatever challenges come my way.

From there, I set out to create a strategy for winning the day. I ask myself, "What do I need to do to make this a successful, fulfilling day? What are my priorities, my must-dos, my opportunities for growth and impact?"

I break it down into manageable pieces. If I can win the morning, then I can win the afternoon. If I can win the afternoon, I can win the evening. And if I can win the evening, then I've won the day.

But winning the day isn't just about checking things off a to-do list. It's about being intentional with my time and energy. It's about focusing on the things that truly matter, the things that align with my values and purpose.

I learned this lesson the hard way. For too many years, especially in my forties and fifties, I found myself chasing after the wrong things—money, frivolous relationships, material possessions. I was busy, but I wasn't productive. I was going through the motions, but I wasn't growing.

Looking back, I realize that I wasn't being strategic about my time. I was letting life happen to me, rather than intentionally shaping my experiences and growth. This realization reminds me of a profound quote from Winifred Gallagher's book *Rapt*: "Your life—who you are, what you think, feel, and do, what you love—is the sum of what you focus on."

This simple yet powerful statement encapsulates a fundamental truth about human existence. We become what we consistently give our attention to. Our focus shapes not just our experiences, but our very identity. If we spend our days scrolling through social media, gossiping, or fixating on negative news, that's what our life becomes. On the other hand, if we direct our attention toward learning, personal growth, meaningful relationships, and purposeful work, we cultivate a rich, fulfilling life.

Understanding this principle was a game changer for me. It made me realize that winning each day isn't just about being busy or productive—it's about being intentional with our focus. It's about consciously choosing what we give our attention to, knowing that these choices compound over time to shape the trajectory of our lives.

This insight led me to completely reframe how I approach each day. Now I understand that time management is really attention management. It's not just about allocating hours, but about directing my focus toward the things that truly matter, the things that align with my values and long-term goals.

Now I know better. I understand that time is our most precious resource, and that how we spend it—what we choose to focus on—determines the quality and meaning of our lives. I've learned to structure my days around four key pillars: energy management, time management, environmental management, and productivity.

I start by focusing on my energy. I pay attention to the people, activities, and situations that fuel me, that bring me joy and inspiration. I prioritize self-care, making sure to get enough sleep, eat well, and exercise regularly. I set boundaries around my time and attention, learning to say no to the things that drain me or distract me from my goals.

Next, I'm intentional about my environment. I create spaces and surround myself with people who support my growth and well-being. I'm mindful of the messages and influences I allow into my sphere, choosing to fill my mind with positive, uplifting content rather than negativity or gossip.

Of course, productivity is important. But I've come to see it as a by-product of managing my energy, time, and environment effectively. When I'm focused and purposeful about those things, the results tend to take care of themselves.

Part of that focus comes from a commitment to what I call "think time"—dedicated space in my day for reflection, strategic planning, and self-assessment. It's a chance to have a deep, honest conversation with myself, to ask the hard questions and wrestle with big ideas.

A former colleague at Nike, Charlie Denson, once posed a powerful question to our team: "Would we be better off doing twenty-five things good or doing six things great?" That question has become a guiding light for me, a reminder to prioritize quality over quantity, depth over breadth.

Winning the day, I've learned, is about making tough choices. It's about having the discipline to say no to the things that don't align with your values and vision, in order to say yes to the things that do. It's about being willing to let go of busyness and distractions in order to focus on true productivity and impact.

But more than anything, winning the day is about the cumulative power of small, consistent actions. It's about the compound effect of showing up and giving your best, day after day, year after year. As Michael put it, "I just think that I had the ability to work hard every day long after most people stopped showing up."

That daily dedication, that relentless commitment to excellence—that's what separates the good from the great, the successful from the truly iconic.

One of my best friends in life, and one of the most intriguing people I know, is the college basketball coach Buzz Williams. Buzz has a saying that perfectly encapsulates this philosophy: "The best thing we do is every day, and the hardest thing we do is every day."

Buzz elaborates, "[Practice] proves who's an Every Day Guy. And if you're not an Every Day Guy, it doesn't mean we love you less, it just means you're going to have to sit over there on the side. You have to be Every Day. . . . There's no, 'We'll do it tomorrow.' No. We're doing it today. . . . You gotta do it every day. And if you can't do it every day, then you're going to struggle because it is every day."

Buzz's words highlight a profound truth about the nature of success and achievement. The more you do something, the better and better you become at it, but the repetitive nature can make it harder and harder to keep doing it.

But that's the price of greatness. That's the sacrifice required to truly win the day, every day. It's not glamorous. It's not always exciting. But it's necessary. It's the foundation upon which all lasting success is built.

I talked to the players at the University of Kentucky when John Calipari was the head coach. At one point, I asked one of the guys, "What is it that you want to do with the rest of your life?"

He replied, "I want to play in the NBA and I want to be one of the best players in the NBA."

I looked at him and said, "Let me ask you a question. What is it that you're willing to sacrifice to do that?"

He was stunned. "What do you mean?" he asked.

I told him, "You're going to have to make some sacrifices. In your game. In your life."

I always try to find out from people how much they are willing to sacrifice to be great. Because that's what it takes.

And that is my challenge to you. Win the day. Not just today, but every day. Wake up each morning and choose happiness, choose intentionality, choose growth. Be strategic about your time, your energy, your environment, your productivity. Have the courage to focus on a few things and do them exceptionally well.

Because when you do—when you commit to the daily discipline of winning each moment, each interaction, each opportunity—you set yourself up for a lifetime of impact and fulfillment. You tap into the power of compound growth, the magic of consistency and persistence.

You become the kind of person who doesn't just talk about success, but embodies it. The kind of leader who doesn't just inspire others, but equips them to win their own days. The kind of difference-maker who leaves a legacy not of grand accomplishments, but of daily devotion to excellence and service.

Remember, while creating order in chaos is about building systems to navigate life's complexities, winning the day is about the immediate actions and choices you make right now. It's about the power of the present moment and how you choose to use it. Every day presents us with countless opportunities to move closer to our goals, to be better than we were yesterday. Your job is to seize those opportunities, one day at a time.

So ask yourself: What can I do today to be better than I was yesterday? What small victory can I achieve in the next hour, the next minute? How can I make the most of this moment right in front of me?

That is what it means to win the day. That is what it takes to achieve true greatness.

So go out there and get after it. Embrace the challenge, the opportunity, the gift of each new day.

Be Every Day.

Win the day.

To Reach Your
Outer Limits

The art of competing, I'd learn from track, was the
art of forgetting. . . . You must forget your limits.
You must forget your doubts, your pain, your past.

—PHIL KNIGHT

Nike lives by what we called the "footwear calendar." It's a
meticulous schedule, mapping out an entire year of shoe
designs and releases. The footwear team works more than
a year in advance, carefully crafting each design for specific moments in the basketball season.

One day in 2008, we were in a meeting with Kobe Bryant,
showing him the shoe and the color variations the team had designed for him. There were designs planned for different moments
throughout the season: the preseason, the first game of the season,
the All-Star game, and so on.

The silhouette was a high-top, which had been the standard in
basketball shoe design for as long as I'd been alive. Underneath
the ubiquity of high-tops was the assumption that they provided
better ankle support. This seemed so obvious that no one ever
stopped to question it.

As we went through the designs with Kobe, I could tell he wasn't saying what was on his mind. He just had that look on his face—not boredom or like he wasn't interested, but like he wanted to say something but just didn't quite know how to say it.

Beyond that, I couldn't tell whether he was mad or disappointed or getting ready to go back to Adidas. I felt uneasy. This was Kobe Bryant. If he wasn't happy or wanted to leave Nike, we had a big problem. He eventually let it out: "You need to make this a lower-cut shoe, or I'm not wearing it." It was a shocking thing to say. It didn't occur to anyone to explain what, again, was so obvious: all basketball shoes are high-tops. It followed that there was no conceivable market for low-top basketball shoes. Not to mention the footwear calendar. The shoes were days away from going into production. It didn't seem possible to design a whole new shoe to be ready for Kobe's upcoming season. "That's your problem," he said. "I want to wear a lower-cut shoe."

The time needed to do something has a funny way of expanding or compressing into the space you need it to fit. We liked our footwear calendar, but we needed Kobe to be happy. The design team worked with him, and "he point-blank said, 'I want the lowest, lightest-weight basketball shoe ever,'" one of the Nike sneaker designers, Eric Avar, would later recall.

After a bad ankle sprain a few years earlier, Kobe set himself on a mission to learn more about ankles. After researching and discovering that tap dancing was one of the best ways to build ankle strength, he found a studio and took up tap dancing. He continued to try to understand how to strengthen his body and get the most out of it, and eventually he noticed: Soccer and basketball involve many similar movement dynamics. Both sports require agility, quick changes in direction, cutting, jumping (in soccer, for a header), and a mix of sprinting and slower, more controlled movements.

So why were all basketball shoes high-tops and all soccer cleats low-tops? Could it be that the high-tops paradoxically cause ankle problems as they prevent mobility?

Kobe brought these questions to Nike's sneaker designers. He was convinced that high-tops were limiting mobility rather than helping it, and that low-tops would allow him to move more naturally, more responsively. He thought they would give him a split-second advantage in changing directions and a fractionally higher vertical. And he knew that split seconds and fractional improvements, at the highest level, are the dividing line between winning and losing championships.

Still, it was a radical idea that went against decades of accepted wisdom in basketball shoe deign. So the Nike sneaker designers had their reservations. But brought along by Kobe's convictions, they designed the Nike Zoom Kobe IV, the lowest and lightest basketball sneaker we had ever made.

The Kobe IV was a trailblazer. As Kobe wore it throughout his MVP 2008–2009 season, it turned out that there was a market for low-tops. Footwear stores around the world couldn't keep the shoe in stock. It wasn't just because Kobe was wearing it. It was because he was right: players raved about what the lightweight, low-cut shoe did for their speed and agility. The success of the shoe on and off the court led other shoe companies to soon follow suit, and now low-top basketball shoes make up a significant portion of Nike's footwear calendar.

At the time of the initial meeting in 2008, Kobe was twelve years into his NBA-career—at that point a ten-time All-Star with three NBA championships.

Most people who have that kind of success get very protective of the things that seemed to have gotten them there. Not just in sports. The screenwriter clings to the software with which they wrote their award-winning movie. A top chef won't work without their trusty old knives.

It's a strange kind of self-sabotage in which one inadvertently restricts their growth by limiting their potential to grow. So attached to the tools, habits, and processes that worked in the past, they stay stuck in that past. They close themselves off from looking for the potential in alternatives that just might make them better.

And then there are people like Kobe. People who look for any little way to get any little bit better. People who don't get superstitious or formulaic or married to the tried-and-true or ever insist that the way they've done things is the way they should always be done. People who reach for their outer limits continually and endlessly.

This relentless search for ways to keep getting a little bit stronger, faster, and better, even through unconventional methods, was the reason Kobe was a trailblazer, and not only on the basketball court. He has been cast as a great basketball player, but the Kobe I got to know was an even greater learner. He was constantly seeking out wisdom, whether it was about body mechanics, storytelling, or business strategy. He approached every area of his life with the same drive to learn, to push beyond his current understanding.

At the 2018 NBA All-Star weekend—two years after he retired and two years before he died—there was a seminar featuring leaders and innovators from the worlds of tech and business. On a stage where he was the only athlete, someone in the audience asked, "Kobe, what are you going to do with your life now that you're retired?" And he said, "I want to work to be as good a businessman as I was a basketball player."

That's a hell of a statement. He didn't just set a high bar for himself; he went public with it, putting himself on the spot, just as he always did. It was vintage Kobe—no finish line, always asking, *What's next?* His commitment to being the best version of himself, in every arena of life, was what truly defined him. It wasn't enough to be a champion in one field—he was constantly reaching for his outer limits in all aspects of his life, always seeking out wisdom and pushing for more.

Whenever I'd see him, I'd usually have a book in hand or under my arm, and he would say, "Hold that up. Let me see. What are you reading?" I would show him, and then he'd ask, "Why are you reading it? Have you gotten anything good out of it?" If there were any insights to share, I would tell him what I'd learned. As I spoke, I could see him calibrating, deciding whether it was something he needed to read himself. If he decided it was, he'd go, "What was the title again?"

There will never be another Kobe. Even if it were possible, I would discourage you from trying to become the next Kobe. Become you. That's what you were made for. We study people like Kobe and Jordan to learn how they became Kobe and Jordan. In studying how they reached their very different outer limits, we figure out some of the things we need to do to reach our own.

I was nowhere close to as good as Kobe or Jordan at basketball, but if I think about it at all, I think about how I reached my outer limits as a basketball player. I did all I could to be all I could.

This relentless pursuit of excellence isn't limited to sports. It's a mindset that can be applied to any field, any aspect of life. Take Jimmy Carter, who interviewed with Admiral Hyman Rickover for the navy's nuclear submarine program. When asked about his class rank, Carter proudly said he was fifty-ninth out of 840 students. Then Rickover asked, "Did you always do your best?" After reflecting, Carter admitted he hadn't. Rickover stared at him in silence for a few seconds before asking, "Why not?" and walking out of the room.

The question stayed with Carter, shaping his life and philosophy. He later titled his memoir *Why Not the Best?*, holding himself to a standard of always striving to be his best, not by anyone else's definition, but by his own. That's what reaching your outer limits is about. It's not about becoming the next Kobe or Jordan or Carter. It's about becoming you. It's about doing all that you can do to be all that you can be. It's about doing your best to be your best. It's about reaching *your* outer limits.

For me, reaching my outer limits has always been about expanding my knowledge and understanding, even long after my coaching career had ended. In my eighties, I still found myself driven to explore new frontiers, often sparked by the books I read and the connections they led me to.

You might remember from earlier in this book how a single word—*mastermind*—caught my attention and set me on a path toward an event that transformed the way I thought about learning and growth. That experience wasn't a one-off revelation; it was the beginning of a new phase in my lifelong pursuit of wisdom. It reignited my hunger for learning, proving that no matter your age, there's always more to discover.

Building on the insights I gained from that mastermind conference, I continued seeking opportunities that stretched me intellectually. Every book I picked up, every conversation I had, every experience I immersed myself in—they became stepping stones, each one pushing me a little further past what I once believed were my limits. That's the nature of growth: it doesn't stop. There's always another horizon, always another level to reach.

Reaching your outer limits isn't just about physical feats or career achievements. It's about constantly expanding your mind, challenging your assumptions, and being willing to put yourself in situations where you're not the expert—where you have to stretch and grow to keep up. For Kobe, it was revolutionizing basketball footwear. For me, it was joining a mastermind group decades younger than myself. For you, it might be something entirely different.

This experience reinforced my belief in the importance of lifelong learning. It doesn't matter if you're eighteen or eighty—there's always more to learn, more ways to grow, more limits to push. And often, the key to unlocking these new experiences and insights is right there on your bookshelf, waiting to be discovered.

When I look back on my own journey, I see this principle at work. I was the best basketball player I could be. Later, I became the best executive I could be at Nike. Now I strive to be the best learner and mentor I can be. Were some people much more successful in these arenas? Of course. But that's not who I was measuring myself against. That's not the race I was in, and it's not the race any of us are in.

The real competition, the one that truly matters, is against ourselves. It's about whether we are doing our best with what we've been given. It's about whether we're pushing our own boundaries, reaching for our own personal outer limits.

I wasn't Kobe Bryant on the basketball court or Phil Knight in the boardroom. But I was George Raveling, giving everything I had to be the best version of myself in every role I took on. That's what I'm proud of. That's what I measure my success by.

And that's what I challenge you to do. Don't get caught up in comparison with others. Don't let the success of others intimidate you or make you feel like you're falling short. Instead, focus on your own journey. Are you doing everything you can to reach your own outer limits? Are you pushing yourself to grow, to learn, to improve every day?

Remember, your outer limits are uniquely yours. They're shaped by your talents, your experiences, your circumstances. Your best won't look like anyone else's, and that's exactly as it should be. The question isn't whether you're the best in the world at what you do. The question is whether you're doing the best you can do.

If you're not doing that, *why not?*

To Bring People with You

At the base of leadership, what all great leaders have in their heads and their expressions is the idea that they want to make people and situations better.

—RANDALL STUTMAN

When I first started coaching, I came across an article about a young man named Johnny Jones, who had scored an astonishing eighty-four points in a single high school game. Intrigued, I reached out to his coach and learned that despite his obvious talent, Jones was only being recruited by historically Black colleges and universities. I knew I had to see him play for myself.

After watching Jones in action, I was convinced: he was better than anyone we had on our team at Villanova at the time. We brought him in for a visit, and because we were the only Division I school recruiting him, we were able to secure his commitment.

It didn't take long for me to realize that Jones was likely just one of many hidden gems in the South, where segregation had kept talented players out of the spotlight. I made it my mission to find these players and give them the opportunities they deserved.

I traveled to games in Florida, Alabama, and beyond, often being the only coach from a predominantly white school in attendance. Over time, I built relationships in these communities, and people started reaching out to me directly, telling me about players I needed to see.

One of those players was Howard Porter, a 6'8" phenom from Sarasota, Florida. Like Jones, Porter was only being recruited by Black schools, despite his undeniable talent. I knew I had to bring him to Villanova, and that's exactly what I did.

Jones, Porter, and others became part of a pipeline of talent from the South to Villanova, one that would eventually be dubbed "the Underground Railroad" by a Philadelphia sportswriter. These players helped lead Villanova to the Elite Eight of the NCAA tournament in 1970 and the title game in 1971. But more important, they showcased the incredible potential that had been hiding in plain sight, and inspired other coaches to start looking beyond the traditional recruiting grounds.

Through this experience, I couldn't help but begin to wonder about the untapped potential hiding in places around the world. If there were so many talented players and natural athletes there to be discovered in the segregated South, surely there must be countless others in countries where basketball was still a nascent sport, where opportunities were limited and exposure was scarce.

As I reflected on this, I couldn't ignore the fact that my own journey to success was far from solitary. Throughout my life, I was fortunate to have mentors, coaches, and supporters who saw potential in me and helped guide me along the way. Whether it was a high school coach who took a special interest in my development, or mentors like Coach Al Severance at Villanova who gave me opportunities I might never have had otherwise, I've always been acutely aware of the role others played in helping me reach where I am today.

The journey to success is rarely a lonely one. As we navigate our paths and overcome obstacles, we have a responsibility to reach back and pull others along with us. This isn't just about individual achievement; it's about collective progress. When we bring others with us, we create a ripple effect of opportunity and growth that can transform entire communities. It's about recognizing that our success is interconnected with the success of those around us.

This realization stayed with me over the years, a seed of an idea that would eventually blossom into something much greater. When I joined Nike as their director of international basketball, I knew that it would provide the platform and the resources to build Underground Railroads around the world. We developed the Nike Hoop Summit, an annual event to bring together the top young players from around the world.

The Hoop Summit became a launching pad for countless international stars, including Dirk Nowitzki (Germany), Tony Parker (France), Enes Kanter (Turkey), Luol Deng (South Sudan), Serge Ibaka (Republic of the Congo), Nikola Jokić (Serbia), and most recently, Victor Wembanyama (France).

I'll never forget the 1998 Hoop Summit, when a young Dirk Nowitzki took the court against a stacked U.S. team featuring future NBA stars like Al Harrington, Stromile Swift, and Rashard Lewis.

But Dirk's journey to that game was anything but straightforward. I had first encountered him at a Nike camp in Paris when he was sixteen or seventeen. Despite being on crutches due to a badly rolled ankle, Dirk had made the six-hour drive from Germany just to meet me and show respect. That level of commitment and determination made an immediate impression.

Dirk's coach, Holger Geschwindner, had approached me before the Hoop Summit, telling me about his protégé's potential. But even he admitted that because of the level of competition in Germany, he wasn't sure just how good Dirk really was. When I saw Dirk play for myself, I was blown away—I had never seen a player his size with such a smooth shooting stroke.

What happened next would go down in Hoop Summit history. Dirk dominated the game, scoring 33 points and grabbing 14 rebounds to lead the international team to a stunning 104–99 upset over the heavily favored Americans. It was a debut for the ages, and it put Dirk firmly on the radar of NBA scouts and executives.

Just three months later, Dirk was selected ninth overall in the NBA draft, and he would go on to enjoy a long Hall of Fame career. Over the years, we've stayed in touch. I remember when Dallas won the championship and Dirk was named MVP, he came to Los Angeles to receive an award from ESPN. He called me beforehand, asking if we could meet up. What struck me most during our time together was his humility. Here was the MVP of the league, and he spent 80 percent of our conversation talking about his teammates and coaches, never once mentioning his own performance.

Dirk has often spoken about the impact of our relationship and the Hoop Summit on his career. In his own words: "I've met, of course, lots of coaches in my career. And, you know, they give you some strategic advice and help you out on the basketball floor. But I think when you meet Mr. Coach Raveling, it was always different. It was about improving the human, not only the basketball player, helping you grow outside of the sport and just making you a better human. For the society, it was always about improving, not only on the basketball court but also off the basketball court."

While I'm humbled by his words, I was simply doing my job, and I don't just mean as employee of Nike. People helped me blaze a trail; my obligation is to do the same for others. What I've always tried to do, with Dirk and all the players I've worked with, is focus on improving them not just as basketball players, but as human beings. It's about helping them grow outside the sport, making them better people for society.

This experience with Dirk and the Hoop Summit taught me the power of creating opportunities and believing in people's potential. Sometimes, all it takes is one person to see something special in someone else and give them a chance to shine. This is the natural evolution of being a trailblazer—once we've found our path, we help others find theirs.

But the Hoop Summit's impact goes beyond any individual player's success. It helped to accelerate the globalization of the game, inspiring countless young players around the world to pick up a basketball and dream big. Today, the NBA features players from more than forty countries, a testament to the growing global appeal of the sport and the impact of events like the Hoop Summit in fostering that growth.

In many ways, this is the natural evolution of being a trailblazer. After pathfinding for ourselves, we shift our attention and energy to helping others find their path. Success isn't just about reaching our goals; it's about turning back and helping others along the way. We may use our networks to open doors, offer guidance to avoid unnecessary detours, or simply reassure others that they're on the right path.

Reflecting on my journey, I'm reminded of the profound impact that one person or a small group can have on our lives. Whether it's a parent, grandparent, sibling, teacher, coach, mentor, or even a complete stranger, these individuals play crucial roles in shaping who we become.

We all play these roles in others' lives—whether as family members, friends, mentors, or colleagues. Every day presents opportunities to be a difference-maker:

Help.

Listen.

Encourage.

Share your knowledge.

Make introductions.

Be pleasant to be around.

Be attuned to the needs of those around you.

Be present.

Be kind.

These small actions matter more than we often realize.

Think about those who made a difference in your life—the ones who saw potential in you, who pushed you to be better, who showed up when you needed them most. These difference-makers changed the trajectory of your life. Don't underestimate your capacity to do the same for others.

As Leo Tolstoy wrote, "Just as one candle lights another and can light thousands of other candles, so one heart illuminates another heart and can illuminate thousands of other hearts." This beautifully captures the ripple effect of our actions. Each time we lift someone up, offer encouragement, or help them along their path, we're not merely impacting that one person—we're potentially touching countless lives beyond them. Through even the smallest gestures, we ignite a chain reaction of positive influence.

As you navigate your own path, take time to look back and see who you might help along the way. Use your network to open doors, offer guidance to avoid pitfalls, or simply reassure others that they're on the right track. You may not always realize the impact you are having in the moment. But every act of kindness, every word of encouragement, every gesture of support—they all matter more than you can possibly know.

You never know when a simple act of kindness or a word of encouragement might be exactly what someone needs to hear. You never know when your advice might be the thing that inspires someone to chase their dreams or overcome a challenge. You never know when your example becomes a trail others follow.

So don't forget to look around or behind you every once in a while to see who you might be able to help.

Don't be afraid to share your knowledge, your resources, your time.

Don't be afraid to reach out and check in on others.

Don't be afraid to make a stranger's day.

Don't be afraid to be a positive difference-maker.

Because it's what you were made for.

To Create Order
from Chaos

When you see a successful individual, a champion,
a "winner," you can be very sure that you are looking
at an individual who pays great attention
to the perfection of minor details.

—COACH JOHN WOODEN

At sixty-two, I was tapped to run the second-largest division in a Fortune 500 company, Nike, despite having no prior corporate experience. Initially, I turned the job down three or four times, convinced I didn't have the necessary skills or knowledge. For the first time in my life, I truly doubted my own abilities.

I confessed my doubts to the executive who offered me the job, Adam Helfant, saying, "Look, I think you got the wrong guy. I don't think I can do this. I don't think I have the skill set for it and I don't want to get too deep into this thing and fail and make you look bad."

Adam refused to let me back out.

"You're not getting out of the job," he said. "You're staying in the job. Here's what I want you to do. When you leave the office every day, leave a yellow pad in the middle of the desk, and when you come in the morning, write down the three most important things you gotta get done that day in that order. That day, do not do anything else but the first thing on the pad. And if you get the first one, then you go to the second one. That will put structure to your day, and it'll give you a sense of purpose."

Then he asked me a question that put it all in perspective: "How many people do you think get the most important thing they have to do that day done every day?"

I thought about it for a moment. "Probably very few," I admitted.

"Okay," Adam said, "so every day put your notes on the pages and save them, and at the end of every month you bring them in and I'm going to go over them with you."

That simple system ended up working wonders. It kept me focused on what mattered most and gave me a clear sense of accomplishment at the end of each day. Suddenly, this daunting new role began to feel manageable. The structure Adam provided aligned with my comfort zone, enabling me to tackle tasks effectively. With that framework and a renewed sense of purpose, I felt capable of handling anything.

This experience reinforced a belief that had guided me throughout my life and career: one of our fundamental purposes as human beings is to create order and structure from the chaos of existence. The world we live in is fundamentally chaotic and unpredictable. The path forward is rarely clear or straightforward. There are always obstacles to overcome, setbacks to weather, and unexpected detours to navigate. It can be disorienting and daunting. But in that chaos lies opportunity—the chance to forge our own way, to create meaning and purpose where none exists.

This idea of creating order from chaos is not new. In fact, it's been a fundamental aspect of human thought for thousands of years. I remember coming across a fascinating concept from ancient Egyptian culture during one of my deep dives into world mythology—a subject I'd grown increasingly interested in as I sought to understand different cultural perspectives on life's big questions.

The Egyptians had a concept known as Ma'at, which represented order, balance, harmony, justice, and truth. Ma'at was personified as a goddess but was also understood as a cosmic force that maintained the universe against the ever present threat of chaos and disorder, known as Isfet.

One of the most powerful stories in Egyptian lore is that of Horus and Set, a tale that vividly illustrates this eternal battle between order and chaos. Osiris, the wise and just ruler of Egypt, embodied Ma'at, the divine order that kept the world in balance. Under his reign, Egypt flourished. But this harmony was shattered when his brother Set, consumed by jealousy, murdered Osiris and seized the throne.

Under the rule of Set, the god of chaos and disorder, Egypt was plunged into turmoil. The land turned barren and people suffered as the balance of Ma'at was disrupted.

Osiris's son, Horus, was destined to reclaim his father's throne and restore order to Egypt, ensuring that chaos would not prevail. Guided by his divine heritage, as Horus grew, he understood that his destiny was to challenge Set and bring balance back to the world. The battle between Horus and Set was not just a physical struggle but a cosmic conflict between Ma'at and Isfet. Set fought with unpredictable fury, while Horus relied on strategy and discipline. Understanding that restoring Ma'at required more than brute force, Horus sought to outmaneuver his opponent.

The battle tested Horus repeatedly. He faced setbacks but always rose with renewed determination. Through perseverance and unwavering focus on his purpose, Horus gradually gained the upper hand.

Finally, he emerged victorious. With Set defeated, Ma'at was restored, and peace returned to Egypt.

This myth serves as a powerful metaphor for our own struggles against chaos. We each face our own Set—the forces of disorder in our lives. Like Horus, we often find ourselves confronted by chaos that threatens to overwhelm us. We have to fight to impose order on chaos, to create structure and meaning from disorder.

In our own lives, Set might take the form of unexpected setbacks, overwhelming responsibilities, or the sheer complexity of the modern world. Our challenge, like that of Horus, is to remain focused on our greater purpose, to use our intelligence and determination to overcome these forces of chaos.

The story of Horus and Set teaches us that creating order is not a onetime event, but an ongoing process. It requires vigilance, strategy, and the unwavering commitment to maintain balance in the face of constant challenges. Just as Horus had to continually fight to maintain Ma'at, we too must consistently work to create and maintain order in our lives.

As we look at examples of how this principle plays out in the modern world, we can see echoes of Horus's struggle and triumph. I saw this principle powerfully at work in my friendship with Bob Knight. Bob was famous for his meticulous planning and attention to detail. He'd carry around a stack of index cards in his pocket, each one filled with notes and reminders—practice plans, drills, points of emphasis, agendas for staff meetings. Even when

Bob seemed to be acting impulsively or emotionally, it was all part of a carefully considered approach. There was a method to his madness, an order underlying his chaos.

That lesson stuck with me in my own coaching career. I sought to provide structure and purpose for my players that extended beyond the x's and o's of basketball.

I developed my own system for creating order and imparting wisdom. Before each practice, I would gather the team in a circle and spend five minutes sharing a story or life lesson. These weren't about sports—they were about life. I might share an anecdote about perseverance, discuss the importance of integrity, or explore concepts like empathy and leadership.

After practice, I handed out articles for the players to read. These weren't sports articles either. They might be about current events, profiles of successful people from various fields, or pieces on personal development. The goal was to broaden their horizons, to help them see life more holistically, beyond the basketball court.

This structured approach to mentorship allowed me to impart wisdom and values, even amid the unpredictable nature of a basketball season. I wanted to create an awareness in their minds of other things in life beyond sports, which tends to dominate the lives of college athletes.

Years later, one of my former players told me he had saved every handout in two boxes in his garage. "Coach, you know all those handouts that you gave out at the end of practice?" he said. "I've got every one of them." It made me feel incredibly good to know that these articles had made such an impact, that the players had taken them more seriously than I'd realized at the time.

This innate human drive to create order out of chaos may be

more than just a metaphor—it may be hardwired into our very biology. In her book *Naming Nature*, Carol Kaesuk Yoon describes a fascinating case that illustrates this point.

A British patient known as JBR, after suffering brain swelling from herpes, lost the ability to categorize the natural world. He couldn't distinguish between a cat and a carrot, or a toadstool and a toad. Interestingly, his understanding of nonliving objects remained intact. This case, and others like it, suggests that we possess a built-in neurological mechanism for imposing order on the natural world, one that's crucial to our ability to make sense of our environment.

The reality is that the world we live in is fundamentally chaotic and unpredictable. The path forward is rarely clear or straightforward. There are always obstacles to overcome, setbacks to weather, and unexpected detours to navigate. It can be disorienting and daunting.

But in that chaos lies opportunity—the chance to forge our own way, to create meaning and purpose where none exists. By imposing structure and order on the disorder around us, we can begin to chart a course through the unknown. We can break down big, amorphous goals into tangible, achievable steps. We can cut through the clutter and noise to focus on what really matters.

This, I believe, is one of the highest callings of the human spirit: to be a force for order in a chaotic world, to create structures that allow us and others to thrive and grow. It's not an easy task by any means. It requires vision and discipline, resilience and adaptability. It means being willing to take risks, to step outside our comfort zones, to bet on ourselves even when the odds seem long.

But the rewards are immeasurable. When we embrace the challenge of creating order from chaos, we tap into a wellspring of meaning and purpose that can sustain us through life's trials. We become architects of our own destinies, builders of something greater than ourselves.

As you contemplate your own path and purpose, don't fear the chaos and uncertainty that inevitably lie ahead. Embrace them as opportunities to impose your own structure and meaning. Have faith in your ability to create order from disorder, to find your way through the wilderness of possibility.

Because that is what we are made for.

To be builders and creators.

To shape the raw material of our lives into something beautiful and meaningful.

To create order in chaos.

It is a challenge worthy of the best that lies within us.

To Be
a Blessing

There is a point in every contest when
sitting on the sidelines is not an option.

—COACH DEAN SMITH

When I became the head basketball coach at Washington State University in 1972, I started an overnight basketball camp called Cougar Cage Camp. It quickly grew into one of the most popular basketball camps in America, attracting six hundred kids each summer from not only around the United States but foreign countries too.

As the camp's reputation grew, there was a shift in the conversations I was having with parents. More and more, they started approaching me with a similar request: "I wish you had a camp for girls too. I'd send my daughter. She loves basketball and she's a really good player."

At first, I didn't give it much thought. Girls' basketball wasn't really on my radar at the time. But as these requests became more frequent, I couldn't ignore them any longer. I realized that there was a real demand for a basketball camp specifically designed for girls, and that I was in a unique position to make it happen.

However, starting a girls' camp wasn't as simple as opening registration. There were political considerations, especially with the university's women's basketball program. I didn't want to create friction, so I approached Sue Durrant, the head coach of the women's team, with the idea. While Sue didn't want to run the camp herself, she offered her full support if I chose to do it.

With Sue's blessing, I decided to start what would become one of the first girls' basketball camps of its kind. At the time, camps specifically for girls were rare, especially at the collegiate level. I knew it wouldn't be easy, but I was determined to make it work. The big challenge was hiring staff. Women's sports were largely overlooked and undervalued at the time, so there wasn't a large pool of women's coaches to choose from. And in the summer months, when a lot of college and high school coaches are either out recruiting or trying to take advantage of the downtime, most men's coaches were not eager to coach at a girls' camp.

I started thinking of ways to make it an attractive job.

Over the years, I had built strong connections with many of the top coaches in the country. These were men who had achieved great success in their careers and had a wealth of knowledge to share. I realized that I might be able to tap into this network to create a truly unique and valuable experience for the coaches who agreed to work at the camp.

My idea was to hire one of the big-name coaches in the game to come and spend an evening with our staff, sharing their insights, strategies, and philosophies. It was an opportunity for the camp staff to learn from the best in the business, to pick their brains and soak up their wisdom. And it was a selling point for me. I could tell prospective coaches that they wouldn't just get a paycheck, but they'd get the unique opportunity to spend time with a coaching legend.

I started reaching out to my contacts, and to my delight, many of them were happy to participate. The first year I got Dean Smith, the legendary coach of the North Carolina Tar Heels, who led the program to two national championships and eleven Final Four appearances during his tenure.

He came midway through the camp, on a Wednesday night, when I had arranged a movie night for the campers. While a few chaperones looked after the campers, the camp coaches spent three hours with Dean. For the first hour, he presented to the group and then opened it up to questions, which began a pretty casual couple of hours of conversation.

The staff was buzzing during the session itself, but it carried over into the remaining days of the camp. And after, because people tend to like to tell others about spending time with a legend, these clinics quickly became the talk of the camp. Year after year, it got easier and easier to fill the camp coaching staff. Coaches would come from far and wide just to have the chance to sit at the feet of a coaching giant. Which meant word began to spread about the caliber of coaches who were coming to teach at our camp. By year three, the girls' camp was rivaling the boys' for the biggest basketball camp in the world.

They came from all backgrounds. Some from well-established high school programs. Others from schools that didn't even have a girls' team. I'll never forget a girl named Jeanne Eggart Helfer. She was a gifted basketball player, but also a track and field star who would later go on to just miss making the 1980 Olympic team in the javelin. Jeanne attended our camp multiple times, and given that she was a phenomenal athlete from nearby Walla Walla, Washington, everyone at the university just assumed she would attend Washington State.

Around the time Jeanne was to graduate from high school, Coach Durrant came to my office and told me that Jeanne's family couldn't afford the tuition. This was very common then and it's a problem that continues to this day. At the time, there were no athletic scholarships available for women at the university. When people say dismissive things about women's sports, I shake my head and speak up. Like it was for race for so long, the playing field was not even. Sports are a reflection of the investments they get from the powers that be, and for a long time women's sports got effectively *no* investment.

As that changes—and it is changing, as Caitlin Clark and Angel Reese have shown—people are going to be amazed by what they see.

Anyway, Jeanne's coach asked if I might be able to help in any way. And I said, "Yeah, I'll just write her a check from the camp." And that's what I did. I used the proceeds of the camp to pay for her four years at Washington State.

It was a moment I'll never forget—the look on the faces of Jeanne and her family when we told them that Jeanne would be receiving a full scholarship, the first of its kind for a female athlete at the university. She went on to have an incredible career at Washington State, setting the all-time scoring record for WSU women's basketball with 1,967 points, a record that stood for thirty-eight years. Jeanne's remarkable achievements on the court solidified her legacy, earning her accolades as one of the greatest players in school history.

But more than that, her scholarship represented a turning point—a signal that women's sports mattered, that female athletes deserved the same opportunities and support as their male counterparts. It was a small step in the grand scheme of things, but it was a step in the right direction.

As I reflect on my journey, I'm overwhelmed by the blessings I've received throughout my life. Someone paid for my high school education. I received a scholarship to Villanova—something my grandmother could scarcely believe was possible. At every turn, there were people who saw potential in me and invested in my future.

These blessings weren't just gifts—they came with a responsibility. I knew I could never directly repay those who had helped me, but I could honor their generosity by paying it forward, by lifting others up and bringing them along the way, just as so many had done for me.

There's a story about Ralph Ellison that's always stuck with me. Ellison, the renowned author of *Invisible Man*, was visiting Harvard one evening. As he walked through Memorial Hall, something caught his eye that would change his perspective forever.

On the wall, carved into marble, was a long list of names. These were the names of Harvard students who had given their lives fighting in the Civil War. You can walk in and see them to this day; it's an incredible and moving thing. Ellison later said that the moment he saw those names, he was almost overcome by the weight of it. He realized that these young men—these Harvard students with all their promise and privilege—had sacrificed everything for an idea. They had died fighting for the freedom of people they'd never meet, people like Ellison's own grandparents. These were men who had given their lives to set him free.

Ellison said it hit him like a shock. Here he was, a successful author, living a life those young men had sacrificed everything for. It filled him with what he called a sense of "indebtedness"—a feeling that stayed with him for the rest of his life.

When I first heard that story, it struck a deep chord with me. I found myself thinking about my own journey, about all the people who had invested in me, who had opened doors for me. My high school education, my college scholarship at Villanova—these weren't just strokes of luck or solely the result of my own hard work. They were the result of countless sacrifices, big and small, made by people who believed in a better future.

I thought about my father, working himself to death in a horse stall to provide for me. I thought about the nuns at St. Michael's who had invested so much time in me, preparing me for a world they knew I'd have to navigate. I thought about Father Nadine. I thought about Coach Al Severance at Villanova, who saw potential in me and gave me a chance. I thought about all the people who had fought for civil rights, who had pushed for integration in sports and education, creating opportunities that I was able to benefit from.

Like Ellison, I realized I owed a debt—not just to the individuals who had directly helped me, but to all those who had fought and sacrificed to create the opportunities I enjoyed. And I knew I couldn't pay that debt back directly. Many of those who had made my journey possible were no longer around, or were unknown to me.

What I could do, I realized, was pay it forward.

That's why, when I had the chance to start the girls' basketball camp and to provide a scholarship for Jeanne Eggart, I didn't hesitate. These weren't just nice things to do—they were my way of honoring the debt I owed to all those who had invested in me, all those who had sacrificed for a future they would never see.

It's not about charity—it's about honoring a debt and continuing a legacy of generosity and hope. It's about recognizing that none of us got where we are solely on our own merits, and that we all have a responsibility to pay forward the blessings we've received.

This perspective has pushed me to always look for ways to create opportunities for others, to mentor, to teach, to give back. Because every time I do, I'm not just helping one person—I'm honoring all those who helped me, and I'm continuing a chain of generosity that stretches back through generations.

That's the power of Ellison's realization: we all owe a debt to the past, and the best way to pay it is by investing in the future.

Looking back now, I can see how that girls' basketball camp was a culmination of so many things I believed in: the power of education, the importance of mentorship, the value of investing in people's potential, the responsibility to be a blessing to others, to share the wealth. But when I say "share the wealth," I don't just mean money. While financial resources can be part of the equation, I'm talking about sharing your gifts, your talents, your knowledge, your time, your relationships, your resources.

This idea of sharing what we have, especially our knowledge and wisdom, is not a new one. It's a principle that has been recognized by great thinkers throughout history. I'm reminded of a passage I once read from the Stoic philosopher Seneca, written in the first century. His words resonated deeply with me and have often guided my actions. Seneca wrote: "Nothing will ever please me, no matter how excellent or beneficial, if I must retain the knowledge of it to myself. And if wisdom were given me under the express condition that it must be kept hidden and not uttered, I should refuse it. No good thing is pleasant to possess, without friends to share it."

These words encapsulate what I've come to see as the essence of being a blessing. It's the understanding that the greatest value of our blessings lies not in hoarding them for ourselves, but in sharing them with others. It's the belief that knowledge, wisdom, and opportunity are meant to be shared, not hidden away. And it's the conviction that when we lift others up, we all rise together.

How can you start being a blessing in your own life? It doesn't have to be a grand gesture or a major financial investment. Start small. Start with what you have. If you have knowledge or skills in a particular area, consider sharing that expertise with others—be it through mentorship, teaching, starting a blog, podcasting, or simply sharing your insights when a friend asks for help. If you have resources or connections that could benefit others, use them. Introduce two people who you think could help each other professionally or personally. Donate to a cause you care about, or volunteer your time and energy to support an organization making a difference in your community. Even small acts of kindness can have a ripple effect, inspiring others to pay it forward in their own way.

Most important, approach every interaction and every relationship with a mindset of abundance and generosity. Instead of thinking about what you can gain from a situation, think about what you can give. Look for opportunities to uplift, support, and empower others, even in small ways. A kind word, a listening ear, a helping hand—these simple gestures can make a profound difference in someone's life.

Remember, being a blessing isn't just about money or material resources. It's about sharing all the forms of abundance in your life—your time, your talent, your compassion, your influence. It's about recognizing that we are all interconnected, and that when one of us rises, we all rise.

WHAT YOU'RE MADE FOR

Start now. Get in the habit. Look for one small way you can be a blessing in your own life and in your community. And trust that every act of kindness, every investment in someone else's potential is planting a seed that will bear fruit in ways you can't possibly imagine.

That's the power of being a blessing. It's not just a philosophy or a strategy. It's a way of living, a way of being in the world. And it's something each and every one of us can embrace, no matter our circumstances or our station in life.

Because ultimately, that's what I believe we are all called to do:

To use our talents, our resources, and our influence to lift up those around us.

To help others reach their full potential.

To add value.

To leave things a little better than we found them.

To create a world of greater abundance, greater opportunity, and greater possibility for all.

And I believe that's a principle we can all embrace, no matter who we are or what we do. We all have something to give, something to share. And when we do, when we use our blessings to bless others, that's when we truly fulfill our purpose in this world.

You've been blessed. Now be a blessing.

To Grow a
Coaching Tree

A life is not important except in the
impact it has on other lives.

—JACKIE ROBINSON

As I reflect on my career, one of the most rewarding aspects has been watching those I've mentored go on to achieve success in their own right.

In the world of sports, there's this idea of a "coaching tree" to represent the lineage of a coach, showing how their former assistants, executives, and players go on to become successful and develop the next generation.

Consider Andy Reid as an example. His career as an NFL head coach is nothing short of legendary, with over two hundred career wins and multiple Super Bowl victories. Reid's success on the field has solidified his place as a future Hall of Famer, marking him as one of the most accomplished and innovative coaches in football history.

However, what makes Reid's legacy even more impressive is the number of assistant coaches who have gone on to achieve remarkable success in their own right after working for him. John Harbaugh, who began his NFL career under Reid with the Philadelphia Eagles, became the head coach of the Baltimore Ravens in 2008 and led them to a Super Bowl victory in 2013. Similarly, Sean McDermott, who rose from a scouting coordinator to defensive coordinator under Reid, transformed the Buffalo Bills into perennial contenders after becoming their head coach in 2017.

Doug Pederson, who served as Reid's quarterbacks coach in Philadelphia and later followed him to Kansas City, made history by leading the Philadelphia Eagles to their first Super Bowl win in 2018. Ron Rivera, who was the Eagles' linebackers coach under Reid, became the head coach of the Carolina Panthers, guiding them to a Super Bowl appearance in 2016, and currently leads the Washington Commanders.

The list keeps going. Matt Nagy, who started as an intern with the Eagles and eventually became the Chiefs' offensive coordinator, went on to head the Chicago Bears. Todd Bowles, who was a secondary coach under Reid, later became the head coach of the New York Jets and is now leading the Tampa Bay Buccaneers. Brad Childress was the quarterbacks coach for Reid in Philadelphia before being promoted to offensive coordinator. He later became the head coach of the Minnesota Vikings. Steve Spagnuolo was a defensive assistant under Reid in Philadelphia. He became the head coach of the St. Louis Rams and also served as an interim head coach for the New York Giants. Pat Shurmur, who worked as a tight ends and quarterbacks coach under Reid, went on to become the head coach of the Cleveland Browns and the New York Giants.

In my own career, I didn't think much about growing a coaching tree in my early years. My focus was on the immediate challenges: recruiting, strategy, and game plans. But as time went on, I began to realize that my true legacy wasn't just in the games I coached or the championships I pursued. It was in the people who came through my programs, learned from me, and then went out into the world to make their own mark on future generations.

The concept of legacy can sometimes feel big and lofty. It sounds like something reserved for presidents, titans of industry, or those who make history books. But when you break it down, legacy isn't about the grand gestures or monumental achievements. It's about the small, consistent actions we take every day to invest in the people around us. Legacy is what happens when you plant seeds today, not knowing when or where they'll grow, but trusting that they will.

Throughout my career, I've had the privilege of mentoring some incredible individuals who have gone on to achieve remarkable success. Coaches like Shaka Smart, Buzz Williams, Jay Wright, Doc Rivers, John Calipari, and Leonard Hamilton have worked under me or been influenced by my guidance and have reached great heights in their careers. Mark Edwards, who coached at Washington University in St. Louis, a Division III school, won two National Championships after serving as my assistant at Washington State. Mike Dunlap, who was with me at USC, claimed the Division II National Championship at Metro State twice.

Look, I never got to feel the satisfaction of hoisting a trophy like that over my head, but I saw them do it and all these years later, it means just as much to me. That's one of the things that happen as you get older. Your own success stops feeling so important.

Seeing these men reach the pinnacle of success is deeply gratifying, knowing I played a part in their journey.

One moment that stands out to me is when Paul Hewitt, another of my former assistants, led Georgia Tech to the Final Four in 2004. I was there in the stands, sitting with his wife, and I'll never forget the moment during pregame introductions when they announced his name: "And the head coach of Georgia Tech, Paul Hewitt." Hearing those words, I felt an overwhelming surge of emotion. All the years of hard work, preparation, and challenges we'd faced together culminated in that single moment.

The game itself was intense. Georgia Tech played UConn, and it was a close contest right up until the end. When the game was nearing its conclusion, and Georgia Tech was on the brink of losing, I found myself in the stands, tears streaming down my face. These were not tears of disappointment, but tears of profound satisfaction. Watching Paul lead his team, knowing I had a role in his development, was a powerful experience.

Paul has since continued his coaching journey, making a significant impact with the Clippers in the NBA G League. His leadership and ability to guide teams through challenging stretches have earned him widespread recognition and respect in the league.

Our greatest achievements are not just our own successes, but the successes of those we've mentored and the lives they go on to touch. The time and effort I invested in them proved worthwhile. That's the most meaningful accomplishment I can imagine. And at a deeper level, watching them touch the lives of young coaches and athletes reminds me that coaching trees provide shade for other young men and women we might never meet.

A coaching tree not only reflects the breadth of a coach's influence but also serves as a testament to the enduring value of their philosophies, strategies, and leadership approaches. When a coach's protégés—be they assistants, players, or executives—advance in their careers and achieve success, it demonstrates that the original coach's methods are adaptable, effective, and capable of being applied in various contexts. This spread and evolution of ideas across different teams and organizations validates the original coach's impact on the sport.

Conversely, the absence of a coaching tree or a lack of successful protégés may suggest that the coach's success was highly dependent on specific circumstances unique to them. It might indicate that their strategies and philosophies were not broadly applicable or replicable, potentially calling into question the sustainability or universality of their methods. A robust coaching tree, therefore, is often seen as a marker of true coaching greatness, as it reflects a legacy that extends beyond individual achievements to influence the wider landscape of the sport.

To me, growing a coaching tree isn't about ego or legacy in the traditional sense. It's about responsibility. I've always felt a deep sense of duty to help these coaches grow, to be there for them in whatever way I can. Whether it's offering advice, providing support, or just being someone they can talk to, I see my role as helping them become the best versions of themselves. My goal is to help them grow deep roots so that the branches of their own coaching trees can be strong and vibrant.

At eighty-seven years old, I don't need another dollar. I don't need a bigger car or more accolades. What I need is the opportunity to make a positive difference in people's lives, to help them in any way I can, and to see them succeed. That's what fulfills me.

John Harbaugh, one of Andy Reid's protégés, once said, "What truly matters is the ripple effect—the pebble in the pond and the waves it creates. It's the effect that you have on people. It's what you leave behind. It's the lives that you change."

This sentiment perfectly captures the essence of a coaching tree—it's not just about the direct impact you have on those you mentor, but about the ripple effect that extends far beyond your own influence. The legacy of a coaching tree is about creating a lasting impact through others—touching the lives of people you may never meet and shaping a future you might never see.

A few years ago, I wrote a note to myself on an index card. I'm not sure what prompted me to write it, but the words have stuck with me ever since: "Spend your adult life making people feel special." It's a simple idea, but it captures the essence of what I believe a coach—or any leader, for that matter—should strive to do. It's about more than just winning; it's about investing in people, helping them grow, and being there to celebrate their successes as if they were your own.

That's what growing a coaching tree is all about. It's about planting seeds in the people you mentor, nurturing their growth, and then watching with pride as they go on to achieve great things and plant their own seeds. It's about creating a legacy that extends far beyond your own career, one that lives on in the coaches and leaders who carry forward the lessons and values you've instilled in them.

Not every branch will flourish, and not every person you mentor will go on to become a great coach. Some may not have the temperament, others might lack the drive, and a few will choose different paths altogether. But that's part of the process. The true value of a coaching tree isn't found in perfection; it's found in the effort, the intention, and the commitment to helping others grow, even when the outcomes are uncertain.

In this way, growing a coaching tree is as much about humility as it is about leadership. It's about acknowledging that you don't have all the answers, that your role is to guide and support rather than control. It's about creating a space where others can develop their own voices, their own styles, and their own paths to success.

One notable branch of my coaching tree that exemplifies this philosophy is Nico Harrison, currently the president of basketball operations and general manager of the Dallas Mavericks. Nico's journey from Nike executive to NBA front office leader is a testament to the power of mentorship and advocacy.

Nico once reflected on our relationship, saying, "Coach Rav has been a mentor, but even more than that, he's been an advocate for me. I'm not in the position I'm in right now without Coach Rav." These words touched me deeply, reminding me of the importance of not just mentoring but actively advocating for those you believe in.

He went on to describe how I tried to instill confidence in those I believed in, telling them about their potential and how great they could be. Hearing that from Nico was both humbling and inspiring.

What touches me most is Nico's understanding that my role transcended basketball. As he observed, "Basketball was the vehicle. But the lessons that he taught would last you well beyond your years as a basketball player or as a basketball coach. They're life lessons."

This reinforces my belief that growing a coaching tree isn't just about developing successful coaches or executives. It's about shaping individuals who will carry forward the values, lessons, and wisdom you've imparted, applying them not just in their careers, but in their lives as a whole. It's about the day-to-day impact you have on people. It's about the small, consistent actions, the words of encouragement, the moments of guidance, and the examples you set.

These are the seeds of legacy, and they grow into something far larger than you might ever imagine.

To Be
an Answer

Let me live in a house by the side of the road,
Where the race of men go by—
The men who are good and the men who are bad,
As good and as bad as I.
I would not sit in the scorner's seat
Nor hurl the cynic's ban—
Let me live in a house by the side of the road
And be a friend to man.

—SAM WALTER FOSS

I spend a good part of the day answering calls.

It's a ritual that's become as familiar as my morning coffee. The phone rings, I pick up, and on the other end is a voice I've come to know well over the years—a coach, a former player, sometimes even a rival from my coaching days. They're calling for advice, for perspective, for a sounding board.

One day it might be Shaka Smart on the line, pausing game film to ask about managing his bench. We talk about treating the bench as a classroom, emphasizing the importance of clear communication and defined roles. I can almost hear the gears turning in his head as he processes the advice.

Another day it might be Buzz Williams looking for guidance on building relationships with administration. I think back to my own experiences, the lessons I learned about the importance of connecting with athletic directors and university presidents. "It's about showing them how you can support their vision," I tell him. "It's about being proactive, not just reactive."

Then there's Jay Wright, seeking advice on dealing with boosters. Doc Rivers, looking to talk through a tough loss. Tom Izzo, reminiscing about old Big Ten battles. The list goes on and on.

These conversations, these daily interactions, are the lifeblood of the relationships I've cultivated over the years. They're the steady drip of wisdom, experience, and mutual support that nourishes the roots of our familial relationships, our friendships, and our coaching trees. It's not about grand gestures or formal mentoring sessions; it's about being there, day in and day out, offering a word of encouragement here, a piece of advice there, helping others grow and become better human beings.

Like a garden that needs tending, these relationships require constant care and attention. Each call, each shared insight, is like watering a seedling, helping it grow stronger and more resilient. Over time, these small, consistent acts of support create a network of thriving, interconnected professionals who can weather any storm and reach new heights in their careers.

What strikes me in our conversations is that we rarely discuss x's and o's. Instead, the focus is on the human side of coaching—the relationships, responsibilities, and pressures that come with the territory. Over the years, countless coaches have reached out when they're on the brink of taking their first head coaching position. I hear the excitement in their voices, but also the fear. They know it's a big step, a huge responsibility.

"Take your time," I tell them. "Make sure it's the right fit, not just for your career, but for your life. And when you take the job, build those relationships from day one—with your staff, your players, the administration. Those relationships will sustain you through the tough times."

As I reflect on these interactions, I realize what I'm really doing is being an answer. Each time the phone rings, it's not just a call for advice—it's life asking me a question: "How can you help this person in this moment?" And my response, my answer, is to use my knowledge, my relationships, and my insights to help them navigate challenges and seize opportunities. I'm connecting dots, bridging gaps, and offering solutions when they're needed most. In many ways, this is the ultimate expression of what it means to be a true friend.

This idea of being an answer is not just a metaphor—it's a way of life that resonates deeply with the philosophy of Viktor Frankl, the renowned psychologist and Holocaust survivor. In his seminal work, *Man's Search for Meaning*, Frankl challenges us to reframe how we think about purpose and meaning in life. He writes that the age-old question "What is the meaning of life?" is not one we ask—it's one we answer.

We need to stop asking about the meaning of life, Frankl argues, and start recognizing that life is the one asking us the questions—every day, every hour. "Our answer must consist, not in talk and meditation, but in right action and in right conduct."

Frankl's words cut to the heart of what it means when I say that we're here to be an answer. Every situation, every interaction, every challenge is life asking us a question. How we respond—how we choose to act—*is* our answer. When I pick up the phone and listen to a coach in need, life is asking me, "How will you use your experiences to guide and support this person?" My job is simply to answer well, with the right action and the right conduct.

This perspective shifts our focus from what we can get from life to what we can give. It challenges us to see every interaction, every challenge, every opportunity as a chance to respond to life's questions with our best selves. As Frankl further explains, "Life ultimately means taking the responsibility to find the right answer to its problems and to fulfill the tasks which it constantly sets for each individual. These tasks, and therefore the meaning of life, differ from man to man, and from moment to moment."

Being an answer requires us to be dynamic, to be able to adapt to each new situation we encounter. Sometimes, being an answer might mean offering advice to a young coach grappling with a difficult decision. Other times, it might mean simply being present and listening when someone needs to be heard. And sometimes, it means having the courage to speak honestly, even when it's difficult. The key is to remain attentive to the questions life is asking us and to respond with intentionality and care.

As we cultivate this mindset, we begin to see opportunities to be an answer everywhere. We recognize that even in our most challenging moments, we have the power to choose our response, to be the answer that the situation calls for. This doesn't mean we'll always have the perfect solution, but it does mean that we're committed to showing up, engaging fully with life's questions, and offering our best selves in response.

We were made to be answers in our families, offering support and understanding when it's needed most. We were made to be answers in our workplaces, bringing fresh perspectives and innovative solutions to challenges. We were made to be answers in our communities, identifying needs and mobilizing resources to address them. This commitment to serving others, to being a force for good in the lives of those around us, is at the heart of what it means to be an answer.

One thing I always tell young coaches is to build meaningful relationships with the athletic director and the president of the school early on. I advise them to call the president and request a short meeting. During this meeting, they should say, "I just wanted to find out how I can help you and your job as the president." This gesture often surprises them and helps build a solid relationship. In college athletics, it's crucial to have strong relationships with the athletic director and the president because they have significant influence over your career.

The beauty of being an answer is that it's accessible to all of us. You don't need a certain job title, a specific set of skills, or a particular background. You just need to be willing to pay attention, to care, and to act. Every situation, every relationship, and every challenge life presents is an opportunity to respond, to bring your unique perspective and experience to bear in ways that only you can.

Remember, we weren't put on this earth to simply seek out meaning. Instead, life is asking something of us, every day, in every moment. We were made to create meaning through our actions, through the ways we respond to the questions life presents. We were made to make a difference, to add value, and to be the solution someone is seeking. In every challenge, every opportunity, life is calling for our best answer—our actions, not just our thoughts.

In every interaction, every situation, you have the chance to fulfill this purpose.

It's not about finding the meaning of life in some abstract

sense. It's not about searching for it in some distant place or waiting for some grand revelation. It's right where you are. It's Every Day. It's in the choices you make, the challenges you face, the calls you answer, and the opportunities you seize.

The meaning is in the here and now, in the way you navigate the complexities of your relationships, your work, and your personal growth. It's about recognizing that each situation, no matter how mundane or challenging, is an invitation to create meaning through your actions, to be the answer that life is seeking.

Every day, in every moment, life is asking you a question. It's asking how you will respond to the circumstances that come your way. Will you bring your best self to the table? Will you engage with the people around you with empathy and understanding? Will you act with integrity, even when no one is watching?

The meaning is in the here and now, in the way you navigate the complexities of your relationships, your work, and your personal growth. It's about recognizing that each situation, no matter how mundane or challenging, is an invitation to create meaning through your actions, to be the answer that life is seeking.

This is what you are made for.

To meet life's questions with purpose.

To create meaning through your responses.

To be an answer.

To Be
a Good Steward

Life's most persistent and urgent question is,
"What are you doing for others?"

—MARTIN LUTHER KING JR.

I was sitting in the living room of one of my recruits, Mark Boyd.
He was a talented kid from Stone Mountain, Georgia, and I
knew he could be a real asset to our program. But as I stood up
to leave, his mother, Betty, looked me straight in the eye and said
something that would stick with me for the rest of my career.

"Coach Raveling," she said, her voice firm but full of emotion,
"I want to tell you something. Look at me." I met her gaze, and
she continued, "I'm sending you my child. Now, I don't want no
foolishness out of you."

I knew exactly what she meant: She had spent her adult life
trying to raise this child. She wasn't about to have me mess it up.

In that instant, I realized that my primary responsibility wasn't
just to rack up wins or build a prestigious program. Mrs. Boyd
was entrusting me with something far more precious: the future
of her son. She was looking to me to be a mentor, a role model, an

ally in the work of raising him into the man she knew he could become. This was about more than basketball. This was about stewardship.

Stewardship, as I came to understand it, is the profound responsibility of being entrusted with the care and development of another person's well-being, growth, or potential. It's a role that goes beyond simply serving others in the moment; it involves a long-term commitment to nurturing and guiding someone toward their best possible future. While service is about addressing immediate needs, and being a blessing can involve broad acts of kindness and generosity, stewardship is about a deeper, ongoing responsibility. It's about being a caretaker of someone's potential and growth, ensuring that what is entrusted to you is not only maintained but cultivated to reach its fullest expression.

This concept of stewardship would come to define my approach to coaching and mentoring throughout my career. But perhaps the most profound example of this came years later, in the summer of 1984.

As an assistant coach for the U.S. Olympic basketball team, I had a front-row seat to the emergence of a young man named Michael Jordan. Fresh out of the University of North Carolina, Jordan was already making waves in the basketball world. His talent was undeniable, but what struck me most was his fierce competitive drive and his magnetic personality.

As the Olympics concluded and Jordan prepared to enter the NBA, I watched as the biggest names in athletic footwear vied for his endorsement. Two stood out as clear front-runners: Converse and Adidas.

Converse had a stranglehold on the basketball market at the time. They were the official shoe of the NBA and boasted endorsements from basketball legends like Larry Bird, Magic Johnson, and Isiah Thomas. Moreover, Jordan had worn Converse throughout his college career and during the 1984 Olympics.

Adidas, while not as dominant in basketball, had a strong international presence. More important, Jordan loved Adidas. "I was fixed on Adidas 110 percent," Jordan said. "My favorite shoes were Adidas."

And then there was Nike, a relative upstart in the basketball world.

I had a long-standing relationship with Nike, having coached teams sponsored by them for years. I believed in their vision and their potential to revolutionize the sports marketing landscape. But more than that, I had a deep, almost inexplicable feeling that Nike was the right fit for Michael.

Over the course of the Olympics, Michael and I developed a special bond. It wasn't a formal mentorship or a coach-player relationship in the traditional sense. It was more organic, a natural connection forged through countless hours of practices, games, and conversations. At some point I began to bring up the idea of signing with Nike, but each time, he would brush it off. "Coach, I'm telling you, man, it's a waste of time," he'd say. "I'm going to be an Adidas guy."

But I persisted. The situation came to a head during the 1984 Olympics. We were in Los Angeles for the games, and I had been quietly advocating for Nike throughout our time together. Some days, when Michael would get frustrated with my persistence, he'd say, "Coach, will you leave me alone about Nike? I told you I'm going with Adidas. And whatever contract Nike offers me, I'm going to give straight to Adidas. They'll match it, and I'm going with them. I'm trying to be as honest with you as I can."

Despite his resistance, I kept at it. Then, after the pool play and before we headed into the medal round, I received a call from Sonny Vaccaro, a key figure at Nike. "Hey," Sonny said, "is there any way you can get Michael to come over and meet me in Santa Monica?"

Now, if you've seen the movie *Air*, you might be familiar with this part of the story. But let me tell you: Hollywood got it wrong. In the movie, Sonny Vaccaro, played by Matt Damon, pulls me into the mix, almost as if he's trying to convince me to help him get Michael to give Nike a chance. In reality, I had been advocating for Nike the entire time. I had already spent months planting the seeds, trying to get Michael to see the potential in signing with Nike. I was relentless because I believed in Nike's vision for the future and their commitment to supporting athletes like Michael in a way no other company would.

The movie shows Sonny and me having a conversation in a bar, where I tell him about Michael's preference for Adidas and his desire for a Mercedes-Benz 380SL. It even has me mentioning that I have a copy of Dr. Martin Luther King's "I Have a Dream" speech as a way to inspire Sonny.

But that's not how things went down.

Here's what actually happened.

When I first asked him to come with me to meet Sonny in Santa Monica, Michael wasn't having it. As he'd been saying the whole time, he wasn't interested in Nike. His mind was made up about Adidas, and he couldn't see the point in wasting time on a meeting. He was set on his path.

"Coach, I'm telling you, it's a waste of time," he said. "I don't want to meet with them. I'm not going with Nike."

But I wasn't ready to give up. I had been working on him for months, and I knew that if I could just get him to the meeting, if he could hear what Nike had to offer, things might change. So I pressed him one last time.

"Look, Mike," I said, "just come with me this once. If you don't like what they have to say, I'll never bring it up again. But you owe it to yourself to hear them out."

He gave me that look, the one that told me he was ready to be done with the conversation. "Okay, Coach," he finally said. "I'll go, but I'm doing this just for you, and after that, I'm done with it. And you've got to promise me you'll leave me alone about it."

I promised.

So, on our day off, I drove Michael to Tony Roma's, a barbecue joint in Santa Monica, where we met with Sonny. It wasn't some casual bar chat between just Sonny and me, as the movie portrays. It was a formal meeting, and Michael was there, reluctantly, mostly to get me off his back about Nike.

But once we sat down, it quickly became clear that this wasn't going to be just another pitch. Nike wasn't playing by the same old rules. Their proposal would fundamentally alter the course of sports-marketing history.

While Michael—and Adidas—was assuming the deal would come down to a dollar amount, Nike was thinking differently. They proposed a revolutionary concept: the creation of a signature shoe line built entirely around Michael: the Air Jordan.

It was a bold, innovative move that signaled a hunger and a competitive spirit and appealed to Michael's competitive nature.

But true to his word, Michael gave Adidas a chance to match. "I went back to Adidas," he would later recall, "and said, 'Look, this is the Nike contract. If you come anywhere close, I'll sign with you guys.'"

Adidas, however, wasn't prepared to match Nike's innovative offer. They were stuck in a traditional mindset, focusing on the financials rather than the potential for something truly ground-breaking. "At that time, Adidas was a European brand that really didn't make a strong push for the United States, and they didn't feel that it was worth it," Jordan explained.

In the end, Michael's decision was easy. He signed with Nike merely because of Adidas's inability to see beyond the numbers.

The Air Jordan 1 was released to the public on April 1, 1985. The deal far exceeded expectations, generating $126 million in sales by the end of the year, shattering initial projections. What was expected to be just another sneaker release turned into a cultural phenomenon that redefined not only sports marketing but the entire sneaker industry. The success of the Air Jordan line propelled both Michael Jordan and Nike to unprecedented heights, establishing a legacy that would influence the world of sports and fashion for generations to come.

At the time, I wasn't thinking about a grand business strategy. I didn't imagine that Michael's decision would set in motion a move that would redefine an industry. I didn't look into a crystal ball and see the global phenomenon the Jordan Brand would eventually become. My thoughts and concerns weren't on market shares or brand equity.

Instead, I felt a deeper, more personal sense of responsibility. I felt a duty not to Nike, but to Michael. This feeling wasn't based on any formal authority or assigned responsibility. Michael hadn't asked me to guide his career decisions, and I wasn't officially tasked with managing his potential. But through our bond, through the trust and respect we had developed, I felt a responsibility to be a caretaker of his future, an almost instinctual urge to guide him toward the path that would allow him to realize his potential to the fullest.

This urge wasn't about personal gain or pride. It was about a genuine desire to see Michael succeed, to see him become all that he could be. It was about a feeling of responsibility that I couldn't ignore, a quiet but insistent voice telling me that I had a role to play in his journey.

Looking back, I don't seek to take credit for Michael's success or claim that I knew all along how things would turn out. But what I do feel is a sense of affirmation that my instincts were right. That in advocating for Nike, I was truly acting in Michael's best interests. I believed deeply, throughout that summer and in the years that followed, that Nike offered Michael the greatest opportunity to maximize his potential both on and off the court.

Stewardship goes beyond just serving others in the moment. While serving others often involves responding to immediate needs or offering support in the present, stewardship is about taking a longer view. It's about seeing the potential in someone and feeling a responsibility to help guide them toward it, even when they might not see it themselves. It's about making decisions and offering guidance based not just on what someone wants now, but on what you believe will be best for their future. It's about having the courage to sometimes push against what's comfortable or expected, because you see a greater possibility ahead.

I think that's what Charles Barkley was saying when he was joking about beating me up to take the "Dream" speech. I had been entrusted with something special, and I needed to take care of how it was going to be passed to the next generation.

This approach to stewardship has implications far beyond the world of sports or business. It's a principle that can be applied in our relationships with our children, our students, our employees, or anyone whose growth and development we have a hand in shaping.

As I reflect on my experiences with Mrs. Boyd, with Michael, and with countless others throughout my career, I'm more convinced than ever of the importance of good stewardship. It's a sacred trust, a responsibility to nurture and guide the potential we see in others.

So I challenge you to consider: Where in your life are you called to be a steward? Whose potential are you responsible for nurturing? How can you guide and shape the future, not just for an individual, but for your community and beyond?

Remember, stewardship isn't about control or taking credit. It's about care and responsibility. It's about using whatever influence or insight we have to positively shape the trajectories of those we serve. It's about seeing the best in others and doing everything in our power to help them achieve it.

That's what it means to be a good steward. And that's what each of us, in our own unique way, was made for.

To Change
the World

How wonderful it is that no one has to wait,
but can start right now to gradually change the world!

—ANNE FRANK

I n the spring of 2005, I received a call from my friend Jerry
Colangelo. At the time, Jerry was the owner of the Phoenix
Suns, and he had just been appointed as the managing director
of USA Basketball.

He faced a daunting task: rebuilding the team coming off its
most humiliating performance in Olympic history.

The 2004 Athens Olympics had been a disaster for Team USA.

The team was loaded with NBA stars like Allen Iverson, Tim
Duncan, and LeBron James, among others. It lost the opening
game 92–73 to Puerto Rico, still the largest margin of defeat in
USA Olympic men's basketball history. It was just the third time
the USA Olympic team lost a game. And it was the first loss since
1988, which was the last Olympics in which NBA players were
not allowed to participate. While it was the first time in Olympic
history that a team of NBA players lost a game, it was not to be

the last. They lost to Lithuania and again to Argentina, finishing the tournament with more losses than every other USA team combined.

The media was brutal. Headlines screamed:

"The Worst USA Team in Modern History"
"From Dream Team to Nightmare Team"
"Humiliating"
"Rock Bottom"
"The U.S. Superstars Had No Answer to Inspired Opponents"

The 2004 Olympics was more than just a disappointment—it represented a sweeping, global change. Team USA had long been an unbeatable juggernaut. In the 1992 Barcelona Olympics, the USA's Dream Team won its games by an average of 43.8 points. They were so dominant that head coach Chuck Daly didn't call a single time-out during the entire tournament. Croatia, led by future NBA stars Dražen Petrović and Toni Kukoč, put up the best fight in the gold medal game and still lost by 32 points. This dominance continued in the 1996 Atlanta Olympics. The team steamrolled the competition, winning their games by an average of 31.8 points. They capped off the tournament with a 95–69 victory over Yugoslavia in the gold medal game. And at the 2000 Sydney Olympics, the USA won their games by an imposing 21.6 points on average.

But Athens was different. The world had caught up. The U.S. players, used to dominating with sheer talent and athleticism, looked lost against teams that played with more cohesion, more discipline, more of a team concept. It was a harsh reality check, a sign that the days of easy gold medals were over.

The fallout was immediate and intense. Players and coaches traded barbs in the media, pointing fingers and assigning blame. The chemistry issues that had plagued the team were laid bare for all to see. LeBron highlighted the lack of structure and discipline in the lead-up to the games as a major reason for their poor performance in the tournament. Head coach Larry Brown said, "We didn't get any practice time. They kind of picked the team at random and it was totally unfair." The frustration was so intense that Tim Duncan vowed, "I'll never play in the Olympics again," a vow he kept. Former NBA head coach Doug Collins, a broadcaster at the games, summed up the atmosphere: "It was a disaster. The level of frustration—there were rumblings that [guys] wanted to [go] home before they even got to the Olympics."

For Jerry Colangelo, the task ahead was clear. It wasn't just about assembling a more talented roster or implementing a better game plan. It was about changing the culture of USA Basketball, about instilling a sense of pride and purpose in representing the country.

He knew he couldn't do it alone.

When I answered Jerry's call, he had just taken on the role of leading USA Basketball forward. To begin to figure out how to pave the road to redemption, he was assembling some thirty former Olympic coaches and players in Chicago over a weekend entirely focused on rebuilding USA Basketball. It was held at the National Italian American Sports Hall of Fame on Taylor Street. Michael Jordan was there. Jerry West. Larry Bird. Clyde Drexler, John Thompson, Scottie Pippen, Magic Johnson, David Robinson,

Dean Smith—they were all there, ready to lend answers and insights.

"I appreciate you all being here," Jerry said in the first meeting of the weekend, and then he laid out some harsh truths. "Look, I was appalled by what I saw in Athens. Which is why I accepted this job. We have a stage here to do something very important . . . I'd be foolish not to take your input. I want to use you as a sounding board. I want to hear from each of you."

One by one, the basketball greats around the room began to share their thoughts. There was no shortage of theories about what had led to the Athens debacle—lack of preparation, lack of commitment from players, a sense of entitlement and complacency.

But as the discussion unfolded, a common theme emerged: the game had changed because the world had changed. For decades, basketball had been an American sport, invented in America, dominated by America. But now, it had become a truly global game, played and loved by millions around the world.

"We Americans invented the game of basketball," Colangelo said at one point. "This is our sport. We sent our own players and coaches to teach it to the rest of the world. And now they're trying to knock us off our perch." "No, it's not," Jerry West replied. "It's not America's game anymore. It's a worldwide game." Doug Collins, a member of the 1972 Olympic team, added, "We have gotten so arrogant. We thought, 'It doesn't matter—we can send anybody and win.' Now we know we can no longer do that."

These words resonated around the room. The sport's global growth had brought with it a new style of play. The international game was different—more team-oriented, more focused on fundamentals and ball movement. But the sport's growth also meant that the level of competition had intensified to a degree never before seen. Other countries were no longer just happy to share the court with the Americans—they were coming to win because they had the talent and believed they could.

As the discussion unfolded, a realization slowly dawned on me. The globalization of basketball that had knocked America off its perch—I was partially responsible for that. Jerry said we'd sent our own players and coaches to teach the game to the rest of the world—and through initiatives like the Nike Hoop Summit, I had sent our players and coaches to teach the game to the rest of the world. I'd thought I was working toward my long-held dream of basketball as a global unifier, a force that could bring together young people from every corner of the earth on a common court. I never imagined that I was also setting in motion the very forces that would challenge our dominance.

The conversation turned to what needed to change. There was talk of overhauling the selection process, of building a true national team program rather than simply cobbling together a collection of All-Stars every few years. There were calls for a renewed emphasis on fundamentals, on defense, on the unglamorous but essential elements of the game.

Above all, there was a recognition of the need to foster a sense of patriotism and honor in representing the country.

In the United States, the NBA looms so large that the primary goal for most basketball players is to make it to the pro league rather than represent their country in the Olympics. Unlike in many other countries, where there is a deep-rooted desire to play for the national team, American players traditionally prioritized their NBA careers over international play. As LeBron James explained, "I think as kids in America and as an African American kid, your whole mindset growing up is 'I wanna be in the NBA.'

You don't really understand the importance of playing for your country. It's not preached about, it's not talked about, it's not shown."

Jerry understood that to rebuild USA Basketball, he needed to instill a sense of pride and commitment to the national team, making players view representing their country as an honor, not just another obligation. This required a fundamental shift in mindset. Players needed to recognize that playing in the Olympics wasn't just a personal accolade—it was about being part of something much larger than themselves.

The work to achieve this would begin with hiring the right coach. Jerry solicited advice on potential coaches and compiled a list featuring all the prominent names: Spurs coach Gregg Popovich, Suns coach Mike D'Antoni, Trail Blazers coach Nate McMillan, Duke coach Mike Krzyzewski, Louisville coach Rick Pitino, and Syracuse coach Jim Boeheim. Everyone in the room was given a vote. It came down to Krzyzewski and Popovich. In the end, it was Jerry's call.

Jerry chose Mike Krzyzewski, who had played for Bobby Knight at West Point and turned Duke basketball into an NCAA powerhouse. Despite his impressive résumé, Krzyzewski was seen as a risk because he had never coached professional players and was coming from the college ranks. However, Jerry liked his background, believing that his military discipline and success at Duke University would bring the necessary deep sense of patriotism and discipline to the team.

"All I can say is this: I was hiring my partner for the next three years," Jerry explained. "Coach K was ready to jump through the phone. I had a clear choice in my mind."

With Coach K at the helm and Jerry's vision guiding the program, USA Basketball began its journey of redemption. Jerry implemented a bold new approach, requiring a three-year commitment from players—something many skeptics thought NBA stars would never agree to.

He met with each player one-on-one, explaining his vision and what he expected from them. "The whole thing started with the old-fashioned thing of Jerry meeting with each of these players face-to-face and explaining what needed to be done and what their commitment would be," Krzyzewski said. "A lot of it is just a handshake, looking each other in the eye, and trusting one another."

For the first time in USA Basketball history, there was a true national team. The three-year commitment from both coaches and players allowed for continuity and proper preparation leading up to the 2008 Beijing Olympics. It was a fundamental shift in how the program approached international competition.

In one of the early team meetings, Coach K and Colangelo laid out their vision. Coach K told the players something that would become a cornerstone of the program's philosophy: "You're not playing for the United States," he said. The players looked confused until he explained further. Pointing to a picture of an Olympic gold medal, he continued, "We won't win that unless you are USA Basketball, unless you own it. The guys on Team Spain, on Team Serbia—they own it. We won't win unless we own it."

The players bought into the vision. Dubbed the "Redeem Team," led by team captain Kobe Bryant, along with LeBron James, Dwyane Wade, and Carmelo Anthony, the squad was a blend of seasoned veterans and young talent.

From the opening tip-off, it was clear this wasn't the same

team that had faltered in Athens. They dominated their group stage, winning all five games by an average margin of 32.2 points. Their suffocating defense and high-octane offense overwhelmed opponents, reminiscent of the original Dream Team's dominance.

However, the real test came in the knockout rounds. In the quarterfinals, they faced a tough Australian team, winning 116–85. The semifinals brought a rematch against Argentina, the team that had eliminated them in 2004. This time, the USA prevailed convincingly, 101–81.

The gold medal game against Spain proved to be the ultimate challenge. In a hard-fought, back-and-forth contest, the USA's mettle was tested. Spain, led by Pau Gasol, kept the game close until the final minutes. It was then that Kobe Bryant, embodying the team's newfound spirit, took over. His clutch four-point play with about three minutes remaining helped secure a 118–107 victory.

"When the medals were being distributed, 'The Star-Spangled Banner' was being played, and the flag being raised," Jerry later described, "it was a moment of total fulfillment. Few people in life have the opportunity to have a plan, watch it be executed perfectly, and get the desired result. It doesn't get any better than that."

It was a victory that marked much more than a return to the top of the podium. It signified a rebirth of USA Basketball's culture and ethos. The Redeem Team had lived up to its name, restoring pride and setting a new standard for future USA Basketball teams to follow.

The journey of USA Basketball's transformation offers lessons that extend far beyond the court. When we organized youth basketball camps around the world, facilitated exchange programs for promising young athletes, and shared our knowledge and love of the game with people in countries where basketball was just beginning to take root, we never imagined that we were laying the foundation for a seismic shift in the balance of basketball power.

Similarly, Jerry didn't revolutionize the USA Basketball program overnight. It was a process built on small, deliberate actions that, when combined, created a powerful transformation. These actions—seeking advice, finding the right coach, having one-on-one conversations, paying attention to details—remind us that meaningful change often starts with seemingly insignificant steps.

In our own lives and pursuits, we can learn from this approach. Whether we're trying to improve a struggling business, repair a fractured relationship, or achieve a personal goal, it's the small, consistent actions that often lead to the most significant changes. Seeking diverse perspectives before making a decision. Taking the time for personal, face-to-face interactions in an increasingly digital world. Paying attention to the details that others might overlook. The seemingly small actions—a conversation here, a change in mindset there—can have far-reaching effects.

This applies not just to sports or business, but to all areas of life. A parent taking a few extra minutes each day to really listen to their child, a manager making the effort to personally recognize their team members' contributions, a citizen volunteering a few hours a month in their community—these small actions might seem inconsequential, but they can create ripples that lead to meaningful change.

Changing the world doesn't mean altering the course of history. Sometimes, it means changing our world—our immediate sphere of influence. It could be fostering a more positive culture in our workplace, being a mentor to someone who needs guidance, or simply approaching our daily tasks with renewed purpose and integrity.

The USA Basketball story teaches us that we're capable of more than we often realize. We have the ability to inspire others, to foster unity in the face of challenges, to turn setbacks into comebacks. We can approach our goals with both determination and humility, understanding that how we achieve is just as important as what we achieve.

In our own unique ways, we all have the power to create positive change. It might not make headlines or win gold medals, but it can make a real difference in our lives and the lives of those around us.

We were made to see potential where others see problems.

We were made to unite people toward a common purpose.

We were made to learn from our missteps and come back stronger.

We were made to change the world—our world—one thoughtful action, one committed effort, one transformed mindset at a time. And in doing so, we might just find that those small changes create ripples that reach farther than we ever imagined.

To Live

As a well-spent day brings happy sleep,
so a life well used brings happy death.

—LEONARDO DA VINCI

I n 1994, at the age of fifty-seven, I was driving through the
streets of Los Angeles on my way to pick up a basketball recruit
for USC. It was a route I had taken countless times before, one
that allowed me to avoid the freeway and, as is usually the case in
L.A. when you avoid the freeways, get there faster. As I approached
an intersection, I looked both ways, saw it was clear, and pro-
ceeded. The next thing I knew, a car slammed into me, propelling
my Jaguar into the front yard of a house on the corner.

The impact was so severe that I blacked out instantly. The first
thing I remember is hearing a police officer's voice: "Coach, can
you hear me? Coach?" As I regained consciousness, the severity of
the situation began to dawn on me.

The police arrived, and as they prepared to take me to the hospital, one officer turned to me and said, "Coach, I've been on the
force for twenty-five years. You don't know how lucky you are.

Ninety-five percent of the time, when I get to a scene like this, the person is dead."

I had suffered a broken pelvis, nine broken ribs, a broken clavicle, a collapsed lung, and bleeding in my chest. I spent two weeks in intensive care and a considerable amount of time in the hospital after that. The doctors later told me that when I first arrived, they weren't sure I was going to make it.

The pain was excruciating, but it was managed by the steady stream of medication I was given. What I remember most about my time in the hospital are the endless hours I spent lying in bed, thinking.

Prior to the accident, I had already made the decision that this was going to be my last year of coaching. I hadn't announced it publicly, but in my mind, I was ready to move on to the next phase of my life. The accident solidified that decision. I knew I wouldn't be able to coach that season or the next due to the extensive rehabilitation I would need.

But beyond coaching, I was confronted with a more existential question: What was I going to do with my life? I had been incredibly fortunate to survive an accident that, by all accounts, should have killed me. Why was I spared? What was my purpose going forward?

As I said, the average lifespan that I could have expected when I was born was a little less than half a century. It struck me there, in the hospital, that in more ways than one, I was living on bonus time. I had been given a second chance at life, a second half of life. How would I spend it? What would I have to show for it?

This brush with mortality changed my perspective profoundly. Before the accident, I had been driven by ambition, by the desire to succeed in my career. But lying in that hospital bed, staring at the ceiling for hours on end, I began to see things differently. I realized that life isn't just about achievements and accolades. It's about the impact we have on others, the relationships we build, the love we give and receive.

As I grappled with these questions, I was struck by the outpouring of support I received. The hospital had to implement a visitation policy because so many people were coming to see me. I received a telegram from the governor. John Thompson came to visit. The president of USC checked on me twice a week. Fruit baskets, flowers, and well wishes flooded in from more people than I ever realized I had impacted.

It was during this time that I began to understand the true nature of legacy. It wasn't about the titles I had won or the accolades I had accumulated. It was about the lives I had touched, the people I had influenced in ways big and small.

I thought about all the players I had coached over the years. The young men I had mentored, not just in basketball, but in life. I thought about the colleagues and friends I had worked with, the relationships I had built. And I realized that my impact extended far beyond what I could see from my hospital bed.

It was a humbling and eye-opening experience. I had always tried to live a life of purpose and impact, but lying in that hospital bed, I realized that I still had so much to give. I couldn't help but feel that I had been spared for a reason—that there was more for me to do.

And indeed, there was. What followed was a second act of my life that I could never have imagined. At sixty-two, I took over as director of international basketball at Nike, becoming one of the highest-ranking executives at one of the world's most influential companies. I played a role in signing Michael Jordan and watched

WHAT YOU'RE MADE FOR

as he became a global icon. Awards, accolades, and honors that I never dreamed of receiving came my way, the vast majority after I turned sixty.

But it wasn't just about the professional achievements. It was about the continued opportunity to make a difference in people's lives. At Nike, I was able to mentor young employees, to share my wisdom and experience with a new generation. I was able to use my platform to advocate for causes I believed in, to be a voice for change.

Even now, at eighty-seven, I wake up every day with a sense of purpose. I'm still learning, still growing, still striving to make an impact. Whether it's through my writing, my speaking engagements, or simply the conversations I have with those around me, I am constantly looking for ways to leave a positive mark on the world.

The importance of living fully and leaving a meaningful legacy was brought home to me in a profound way recently with the passing of my dear friend Jerry West. When my wife woke me early one morning with the news, I was overcome with emotion. It hit me harder than I could have anticipated, leaving me in a state of shock and disbelief.

In the days that followed, I found myself needing space to process this loss. I turned off my phone, disconnecting from the outside world for two full days. This wasn't just grief; it was an opportunity for what I call "mind cleansing"—a chance to reflect deeply on my relationships, my life, and the impact others have had on me.

Jerry and I had a special bond, one that transcended our shared love of basketball. He was a greater friend and supporter than many people realized. In the quiet moments of reflection following his passing, memories flooded back. I remembered a moment from our playing days that Jerry had recalled years later—how he had spontaneously reached out to shake my hand and wish me luck as I fouled out of a game. It was a small gesture, but one that spoke volumes about his character.

As I sat with my thoughts, I realized how rarely we take the time to truly appreciate the people in our lives while they're still with us. It shouldn't take a loss to prompt us to reflect on the impact others have had on us. This realization led me to spend days writing, filling nearly forty pages with notes and reflections on the relationships that have shaped me.

In this process of reflection, I couldn't help but confront my own mortality. At eighty-seven, the same age as Jerry, I found myself acutely aware of the precious nature of time. I began to think of life as a basketball game in its final quarter, with just minutes left on the clock. Phil Jackson has talked about how that was a lesson he learned from the great Red Holzman of the Knicks. Phil was on the bench and Red called him over and asked him how much time was on the game clock. Phil, who had been resting or engrossed in the play, didn't know.

"You've got to know," Red told him. "You may be going into the game, and if you don't know the time, you could get us in trouble. Don't let me catch you doing that again."

For me, I know what time it is . . . which is to say, near the end. There's no way around that. In fact, as I said, at my age I'm closer to something like double overtime or extra innings. The question then becomes: How will I use this remaining time? How can I ensure that these last minutes are played with purpose and impact?

This perspective has made me even more determined to make the most of whatever time I have left. I want to invest my remaining days wisely, to continue making a positive difference in the world around me. It's reinforced my belief that we should strive to live in a way that, when our time comes, we can face it knowing we've given our all.

I realize that my readers—you—are probably much younger than me. But the truth is that life, unlike sports, doesn't have a minimum length. All of our lives could be cut short. The buzzer can sound at any moment, as I nearly and dearly learned in that car wreck. So you must be aware not so much of how much time is on the clock but of the fact that each and every second, that clock is ticking, ticking away, ticking off time that does not come back.

In a moment of synchronicity that still gives me goose bumps, just two days before Jerry passed, I had sent him a message. It read:

> I think of you every single day with love in my heart and best wishes for good health and stability. I miss your presence, wisdom, and leadership. Hope to see you soon, my friend. God bless you and your family.

Those words, unknowingly my last to him, encapsulate what I believe is most important in life—expressing our love and appreciation for others while we still can.

This experience has only strengthened my conviction that we must live each day with intention and gratitude. It's reminded me of the importance of telling the people in our lives what they mean to us, of not waiting for some future moment to express our feelings or pursue our dreams. We must live with urgency. We must use what is before us before it's used up.

As I continue to reflect on Jerry's passing and my own journey, I'm more committed than ever to the idea that our legacy is built not in grand gestures, but in the accumulation of our daily choices and actions. It's about how we treat others, the wisdom we share, the love we give, and the positive impact we strive to make each day.

To truly live, then, is to embrace each moment with purpose and appreciation. It's to recognize that our time is limited, but our potential for impact is not. It's to understand that in the game of life, how we play those final minutes can define our entire legacy.

As I reflect on my life, I am filled with a profound sense of gratitude and purpose. I have been blessed with a life that has exceeded my wildest expectations, a life filled with more overtime periods than I can count. Every time I thought the game was over, I was given more time on the clock.

But I have also come to realize that it's not just about how much time we are given, but what we do with that time. We all have a choice in how we live our lives. We can go through the motions, or we can strive to make an impact. We can complain about our ailments, or we can embrace the gift of each day. We can live in fear of our own mortality, or we can use it as motivation to make the most of every moment.

I've made my choice. I don't know how much time I have left, but I know that I will spend it continuing to try to make a positive impact in the world. I will spend it connecting with others, sharing my experiences, and living each day with gratitude and purpose.

Because that, I have come to believe, is what we are all made for—to *live*. Not merely to exist, survive, float, or drift along, but to truly live. To squeeze every ounce of meaning and impact out of the time we are given. To touch as many lives as we can. To study, listen, learn. To keep going, even when the odds seem insurmountable.

As I look back on my journey, from that young boy in Washington, D.C., to the man I am today, I'm struck by how far I've come and how much I've learned. Each chapter of my life has taught me something valuable:

- **TO BE A TRAILBLAZER:** to have the courage to forge new paths and open doors for others.

- **TO LISTEN AND LEARN:** to remain curious and open to new ideas and perspectives.

- **TO SEEK OUT WISDOM:** to actively pursue knowledge with curiosity, embrace diverse perspectives, and step beyond comfort zones for growth and understanding.

- **TO STRUGGLE:** to embrace challenges as opportunities for growth, knowing that the setbacks and hardships we endure shape us and give meaning to our triumphs.

- **TO STUDY BOOKS:** to never stop learning and growing.

- **TO DISPENSE LOVE:** to spread kindness and compassion in all that you do.

- **TO SERVE OTHERS:** to use your gifts and talents for the benefit of those around you.

- **TO KEEP HOPE ALIVE:** to believe in the possibility of a better future, even in the darkest of times.

- **TO BE A FRIEND:** to cultivate meaningful relationships and be there for others in times of need.

- **TO BUILD YOUR TEAM:** to nurture meaningful connections, embrace shared roles and responsibilities, and recognize that success is never a solo journey but a collective effort.

- **TO TELL THE TRUTH:** to live with integrity and speak honestly, even when it's difficult.

- **TO WIN THE DAY:** to approach each day with intention and purpose.

- **TO REACH YOUR OUTER LIMITS:** to continually push yourself to grow and improve.

- **TO BRING PEOPLE WITH YOU:** to lift others up as you climb.

- **TO CREATE ORDER FROM CHAOS:** to find structure and meaning in life's challenges.

- **TO BE A BLESSING:** to use your resources and influence to make a positive difference in the world.

- **TO GROW A COACHING TREE:** to nurture others' growth, celebrate their successes, and build a legacy that transcends your own achievements.

- **TO BE AN ANSWER:** to recognize needs, build connections, and act as a catalyst for positive change by using your unique skills and insights to create value for others.

- **TO BE A GOOD STEWARD:** to foster other people's potential to reach its fullest expression.

- **TO CHANGE THE WORLD:** to believe in your power to make a difference, no matter how small.

- **TO LIVE:** to embrace each moment with purpose, gratitude, and urgency, making the most of our limited time to leave a meaningful impact on others.

These lessons have shaped my understanding of what it means to truly live. They've guided me through the highs and lows, the triumphs and setbacks. And they continue to inspire me every day to make the most of the time I have left.

To those reading this, especially the younger generation, I want to leave you with this message: Your life is a gift. It's an opportunity to make a difference, to leave the world a little better than you found it. Don't wait for some future moment to start living with purpose. Start today.

Here are some steps you can take right now to live more fully:

1. **REFLECT ON YOUR VALUES:** What matters most to you? What do you want your life to stand for?

2. **SET MEANINGFUL GOALS:** Not just career goals, but personal growth goals. How do you want to improve as a person?

3. **PRACTICE GRATITUDE:** Take time each day to appreciate the good in your life.

4. **SERVE OTHERS:** Look for ways to make a positive impact on those around you.

5. **KEEP LEARNING:** Read widely, seek out new experiences, stay curious about the world.

6. **BUILD RELATIONSHIPS:** Invest time and energy in the people who matter to you.

7. **TAKE CARE OF YOURSELF:** Your physical and mental health are crucial to living a full life.

8. **EMBRACE CHALLENGES:** See difficulties as opportunities for growth.

9. **LIVE WITH INTEGRITY:** Let your actions align with your values.

10. **LEAVE A LEGACY:** Think about how you want to be remembered and start living that way now.

As for me, I hope my legacy will be one of inspiration and impact. I want to be remembered not just as a successful coach or executive, but as someone who uplifted others, who fought for equality and opportunity, who never stopped learning and growing. I want future generations to look at my life and see that it's possible to overcome adversity, to reinvent yourself at any age, to make a difference no matter where you come from.

But more than that, I hope my story encourages others to live their own lives to the fullest. To embrace their unique gifts and use them to make the world a better place. To understand that every day is an opportunity to learn, to grow, to love, to serve.

In the end, we won't be remembered for the years we lived, but for what we did with those years. We won't be measured by metrics like wins and losses or successes and failures, but by questions like:

Was he a good person?
Was she kind?
Did he make a positive difference on the people around him?
Did she pursue her unique path with courage and resilience?
Were they a person of integrity? Someone who kept their word?
Someone who told the truth? Someone you could trust?
Did they leave this place a little better than they found it?
Did they really live?

Make sure you do. Make sure you live with purpose.

With excitement and hope and the understanding and the appreciation that every day is an opportunity . . .

To study, learn, listen, love, and serve.

To be a friend.

To reach your outer limits.

To make a positive difference.

To change the world.

To be alive.

Make it count. Make it matter. Make it make a difference.

That is what you were made for.